Sophia Daniel
is an experienced healer and dream analyst. She writes the
dream column in *Prediction* magazine and runs regular
courses on healing development.

Dream Healing

A Practical Guide to
Unlocking the Healing Power
of Your Dreams

Sophia Daniel

ELEMENT

Shaftesbury, Dorset • Boston, Massachusetts • Melbourne, Victoria

© Element Books Limited 1999
Text © Sophia Daniel 1999

First published in the UK in 1999 by
Element Books Limited
Shaftesbury, Dorset SP7 8BP

Published in the USA in 1999 by
Element Books, Inc.
160 North Washington Street
Boston, MA 02114

Published in Australia in 1999 by
Element Books and distributed
by Penguin Australia Limited
487 Maroondah Highway, Ringwood,
Victoria 3134

Reprinted 2000

Cover illustration courtesy PowerStock/Zefa
Cover design by Mark Slader
Design by Behram Kapadia
Illustrations by David Woodroffe
Typeset by Bournemouth Colour Press, Parkstone
Printed and bound in Great Britain by JW Arrowsmith, Bristol

British Library Cataloguing in Publication data available

Library of Congress Cataloging in Publication data available

ISBN 1 86204 459 7

Contents

ENTIRE FORM WITH YOUR PACKAGE TO: **ATTN: CUSTOMER SERVICE DEPT.**
151 INDUSTRIAL DRIVE, SUITE A, BEAVER DAM, WI 53917

Please print Order #, name, address, and zip code
exactly as it appears on your invoice or on the mailing label of your package.

ORDER #: _____

NAME: _____

ADDRESS: _____

CITY: _____   STATE: _____   ZIP: _____

TELEPHONE: (____) _____

* RETURN REASON CODES

A. Arrived Damaged

B. Wrong/Duplicate Order

C. Other

COMMENTS:

MERCHANDISE RETURNED

ITEM #	DESCRIPTION	PRICE	* RETURN REASON CODE	REPLACEMENT REQUESTED *CHECK HERE*

Your account will be adjusted within 5-6 weeks. (Please ignore any bills you may receive for the item you are returning until then.) If you are requesting a replacement, or are due a refund, it will arrive shortly thereafter.

Introduction

Since time immemorial, people of all cultures have been fascinated by dreams and their interpretation. Some of the earliest known dreams come from Egypt and were recorded some 4,000 years ago, long before the biblical accounts of Joseph's and Daniel's dreams were written down. In those ancient times dreams were frequently regarded as messages from the gods, or as oracles predicting the future. But dreams were also used effectively for healing purposes, and still are in many parts of the world today.

In our modern Westernized world, dream healing is a lost and neglected art. However, our full and stressful lifestyles have not only triggered a marked rise in the number of life-threatening 'modern' diseases; they have also led many people to participate actively in their own healing process and to share with the medical profession the responsibility for their return to normal health and well-being. This has led us to take a fresh look at old ideas, resulting in the rebirth of many ancient forms of healing, as well as the advent of modern forms of treatment, including some which may seem downright weird. What is important, however, is that these methods involve the whole person: they require us to participate, to assist with the healing process and even work on our own. This applies very much to the area of dream healing.

Dreams are ourselves talking to ourselves, and when we learn to understand and interpret our personal dream language it becomes apparent that we can deal with virtually all waking problems. There seems to be a part deep inside of us that truly understands all of our needs. To use computer language, it is the HELP button. It is there all the time, an enormous resource, patiently waiting for us to draw on it. We can draw on it through our dreams. Unfortunately, most of the time we forget its very existence and, when we do inadvertently touch on it, its language can be very confusing.

● ●

This book is designed to enable us to hear the messages of our dreams, to understand their import and, hopefully, follow their advice. It describes how the mind works, how it creates for each of us its own personal language of pictures combined with archetypal imagery from our ancestors. Apart from a detailed examination of how the body is used symbolically in dreams to explain illnesses, it avoids long lists of interpretations, taking only the main dream themes.

The book includes a number of practical easy-to-follow dream techniques, such as incubation and lucid dreaming, and shows how we can sow seeds into our unconscious levels to help diagnose the underlying causes of illness. It explains how to remember and record our dreams before they slip out of our minds and why some dreams are so powerful they remain with us all day. It also explains how we translate abstract emotions and ideas into imagery in order to create a storyline, how to understand the messages and answers we receive, and how we can act on them to improve our health and well-being.

1

....

What is Dreaming?

Dreaming is one of the most overlooked areas of human experience and yet, strange though it may seem, much of our highly industrialized, computerized world is the result of dreams. Out of the dream world have come wisdom, art, literature, healing, scientific discoveries, inventions, government policies and battle strategies. In fact, dreams would appear to be the source of unlimited human potential. Yet today the interpretation of dreams is often dismissed as light entertainment, a bit of frivolity that we indulge in when we aren't busy working. As for nightmares, rather than understand them, the sooner we can escape from them the better.

What we tend to overlook is that when we dream we are communicating with ourselves. When we ignore or misunderstand the dream world, we actually throw away amazing opportunities for improving our lives. During a dream, apart from noises and natural physical responses, there is no outside input or interference. The deeper level of the mind can therefore express itself freely, without the imposition of the waking, logical mind. It is similar to the ingenuous self-expression of a young child who is, as yet, unaware of social restrictions. The child freely speaks its mind without fear of chastisement. Similarly our dreams tell us bald truths about our lives. If we pay attention to this 'small voice' and act upon its advice and suggestions, we can discover how to lead healthier and more fulfilled lives.

This book explains how we can learn to do this, as well as how to use our dreams to help heal ourselves physically, emotionally, mentally and spiritually. But first it is important to understand what dreams are, why we have them and what happens to us while we are dreaming.

Sleep Patterns and Dreaming

We spend almost one third of our lives sleeping. For a long time it was thought that the only reason for sleeping was to rest the body. However, modern scientific research has shown that the brain is very active during sleep and that the physical body can be rested without actually sleeping. Now it is thought that we sleep in order to dream.

There are two main types of sleep: deep sleep and periods of lighter sleep combined with rapid eye movements, known as REM (Rapid Eye Movement) sleep. Most of our dreaming takes place in the REM state, when images are usually specific and non-fuzzy. Dreams with a shadowy, inconclusive tone are rarer and relate to deeper levels of sleep.

Sleeping follows a regular pattern which begins with a period of deep sleep during which the sleeper sinks into the slowest level of brain activity for approximately 90 minutes. This is followed by a short period of REM activity before a further return to deep sleep. This alternating pattern continues throughout the night, with the REM periods becoming longer, and is directly related to how we feel on awakening. If the periods of REM sleep are reduced or interrupted, we will probably complain of not having slept well. In reality, however, our tiredness may be attributed to the amount of dreaming we have missed rather than the overall quantity of sleep.

Our modern belief in the essential eight hours sleep per night frequently leads to remarkable stress if it is not achieved, making us toss and turn the night away in endless frustration. However, our bodies are completely aware of our individual needs, be they three hours or ten hours. Once we acknowledge this, the worry is removed – and often the sleeplessness. What is important is the *quality* of our sleep, and this is where our lifestyles tend to interfere.

It is only at the beginning of life that long hours of sleep really are necessary – current research reveals the secretion of the growth hormone during sleep. Moreover, young babies, who spend most of their time sleeping, have considerable periods of REM, which has led some researchers to suggest that dreaming takes place before birth. Since dreaming, sleep and REM are connected, could it be that dreaming is required for the growth process in the womb?

We also need sleep when we are ill, because sleeping is our body's natural response to assist in the repair process. (We need only look at the behaviour of animals when they are ill to understand this.) The healthy functioning of our immune system also relies on deep sleep: bacteria in the intestines produce sleep-inducing chemicals which, on reaching the brain, set in motion a chain of chemical events to produce defensive cells.

Laboratory testing has revealed that dreaming is essential for our health, even though we may never remember the content of our dreams. Experiments involving the deprivation of REM sleep have resulted in subjects experiencing disorientation, depression and anxiety. It would therefore seem that, whether we remember them or not, dreams are an integral part of a process which ensures our continued well-being.

Many of us have had personal experience of thoughts producing physical reactions despite the absence of any kind of physical stimulus. For example, if we have been bereaved, thinking about the lost loved one tends to bring tears to the eyes. Or recalling a particularly funny incident can produce a smile or even laughter. Likewise, remembering a frightening incident can cause fear, with the tightening of stomach muscles and butterflies in the tummy. It therefore appears that as thoughts pass through our minds we continuously react to them physically, the intensity of the reaction depending on the nature of the thought. But because this phenomenon is so commonplace, we only notice the more dramatic occasions.

You can try this out for yourself – just imagine that you are placing a slice of raw lemon in your mouth and sucking it. In 99 cases out of 100 there will be an immediate reaction of the mouth watering, with increased saliva flow, which would be the natural waking response to sucking a lemon. The body has reacted to a thought only. In bygone days when brass bands were a regular feature in our parks, naughty children used to stand in front of the bandsmen and actually suck raw lemons. This would often reduce the band to spluttering silence as the players found the saliva spilling out of their mouths into their instruments.

Exactly the same thing happens when we think of someone who sexually excites us – we experience a sensation of fire shooting through the body. Similarly if we are afraid of heights, just contemplating crossing a suspension bridge can cause sweating or dizziness. Most common of all is that 'Monday morning feeling', when resentment at having to work fills us with gloom and brings tension to the solar plexus. These are all conscious reactions and we can assess them for ourselves. However, there are many others going on just below our surface consciousness which also produce physical reactions – stress and tension, anger and irritation – and affect our bodies in ways which, if unrelieved, can frequently cause illness.

If, as research has shown, the brain is still actively 'thinking' in the REM or dream stage of sleep, could it be that the body continues to respond to thought – that is, dream thoughts – while we are asleep? If so, it would appear that dreams are part of an automatic healing and repairing process, which is why we cannot manage without them. As mentioned earlier, deprivation of REM sleep can have a marked effect on us. Research has shown that it can even result in mental and behavioural abnormalities, such as aggression, disorientation, difficulty in concentrating, hallucinations and sometimes psychosis. It has also been found that the sleeper spends more time in REM sleep following a deprivation period. If this is so, then learning to control and utilize our dreams takes on a new importance for our own health and well-being.

Dream-related Phenomena

It is well known that physical reactions continue while we are in the sleep state. Anyone who has ever experienced a nightmare will understand this only too well. We can wake up sweating, with heart thumping, trying to scream. The body is in a state of fear – the 'fight or flight' state – with our adrenalin pumping. All of this is a reaction to imagery in the mind, not to reality. In the same way sexual reactions are normal and quite common while dreaming. Erections, increased vaginal secretions and orgasms all occur frequently during sleep. Research in this area reveals some interesting facts: during REM or dream periods 80 per cent of men have erections, homosexuals have heterosexual dreams, and paraplegics or quadriplegics, of both sexes, experience orgasm. Of course, there may be a simple physical explanation for this, but nonetheless it is clear that dream thoughts produce responses in the body in precisely the same way that waking thoughts do.

In view of this it is important to understand the difference between dream-induced responses and dream-related phenomena. The latter are natural physical occurrences that are absorbed into the dream. To understand the difference between the two, consider some of the things that can happen naturally when we close our eyes. For example, when we stare hard at something for a few minutes and then close our eyes we have a reverse image on the retina which lasts for some moments. The same occurs if we look out of a window before closing our eyes – we have a photo negative of a light frame with dark squares or rectangles. When our eyes are closed we can also be aware of shadows and variations of light and shade. It has also been discovered that if we close our eyes and concentrate our attention on one spot as though our eyes were open, we begin to see transient points of light – some of which may be coloured – moving and colliding. This phenomenon was researched by Henri Bergson in France around the beginning of the twentieth century. Bergson theorized that these points of light were caused by blood circulation in the retina and that the mind used them to create dream shapes and images while the imagination provided an appropriate storyline.

In the period between sleeping and waking, hypnogogic and hypnopompic images occur (*see* page 37). These images – hypnogogic as we fall asleep, hypnopompic as we wake – can also occur during deep meditation and coincide with periods of deep Alpha-brainwave activity. In this state we may perceive vivid, highly coloured, but seemingly unconnected images. Strangely, we are convinced that we are still wide awake and it comes as a surprise when we realize that this is not the case. We may also experience a sense of detachment and non-involvement. Unfamiliar faces are common, as are disconnected scenes, and the effect can be rather like a bizarre slide show, or like flipping through TV programmes with a remote control. Sometimes the meaning of these images can be extremely profound and visionary, but frequently they appear to have no coherent or valuable message. Hypnogogic and hypnopompic images should not be muddled with hallucinations. The latter occur in a waking state and are a confusion of fantasy images with normal perception.

The dreaming mind can be influenced by a whole series of physical occurrences which can either add to the significance of the dream or just interfere by giving false or distorted messages. It is therefore important to understand something of the workings of the body in the sleep state. Sometimes it is the dream itself that induces a physical response; at other times we tune in to the natural functions of the body and translate them into a dream.

When we enter the sleep state it is perfectly natural for our metabolism to change. Breathing slows down; body temperature, blood pressure and heart rate reduce, and there is a gradual decrease in the cycles of the brainwaves. As we wake, the process is reversed; all these different phases can be translated in the mind of the sleeper as part of the dream.

During certain levels of sleep the muscular reflexes associated with the limbs and throat disappear and the sleeping person actually appears to be paralysed. This condition, known as sleep paralysis, can penetrate the dream state and can also

7

continue into partial wakefulness, which can be very frightening. This often manifests in a nightmare as a complete inability to run, move in any way, or even cry out. We can wake and find ourselves desperately trying to scream or shout for help.

My mother used to have a regular nightmare that illustrates this state. She was lying in a desert, and something was coming towards her. She was terrified because she could not move. All her limbs seemed huge and completely unresponsive. Each time the unknown being came closer, but it never actually reached her. Such dreams are fairly common and usually mean the dreamer is in a situation over which they have no control and which cannot easily be changed.

Catalepsy is a similar phenomenon, except that there is rigidity rather than flaccidity in the muscles, which, together with a greater consciousness of the immobile state, creates an equal feeling of helplessness. In both cases, however, the simple act of opening the eyes seems to bring the body back under conscious control. Catalepsy is often the result of extreme stress combined with incorrect sleeping conditions. A soft bed moulds itself to the shape of the stressed body, thereby allowing the tensed muscles to be accommodated in their rigid state, whereas a hard bed obliges total relaxation in order for us to sleep at all. The following dream illustrates a state of catalepsy:

I dreamed that I was swimming in an endless ocean. There was no land in sight anywhere and I could feel my strength failing. Gradually my legs and feet began to stiffen, then my body, and finally, as I was desperately thrashing with my arms to keep afloat, my arms became rigid too and I knew I was going to sink. Then I woke up, my throat absolutely stiff from trying to shout out.

Another common experience is that of twitching in sleep. Sometimes this becomes a much more pronounced and sudden jolt – the myoclonic jerk – which occurs either on falling asleep or on waking. There are two theories about this: firstly, that it is a sudden contraction of the muscles; secondly, that it is to do with the relaxation of the deeper muscle structure – a sudden spasm as these release when we thought we had let go completely. It is fairly commonplace for people to go through a relaxation process which only involves the obvious external muscles. The deeper layers against the skeleton can remain tensed, taking longer to release. Again the dream mind translates these jerks into the dream. The sensation of stepping off a step into nothingness is quite common, as is walking off a precipice or crash-landing:

I am walking up a spiral staircase in a castle. I come to a door and it is very dark. I open the door and walk through. There is an awful sensation as I step into nothing.

A full bladder is one physical aspect which can infiltrate the dream world in many guises – searching for a lavatory, having to go behind a bush or similar, or simply waking up and going to the toilet. Thus the need to urinate in a dream can be a true physical need rather than a deep suggestion to relieve oneself of something. Enuresis (bed-wetting) mainly occurs in disturbed children, usually when there is an excess of authority. It can also be caused by a weakness in the muscles, which allows leaking of the full bladder when the body lets go of its natural muscular reflexes, as in sleep paralysis.

Sleep-walking and talking occur when we act out a dream. These phenomena indicate that the normal relaxation of the muscular reflexes is not taking place. This is usually associated with times of extreme anxiety and stress in daily life. (Some experts consider the cause to be incorrect firing mechanisms in the brain.) This can manifest in a number of ways, from simply walking round the room or muttering a few words, to loud shouting or singing, or even extremely violent and dangerous actions. Unless the sleep-walker is behaving violently, it is usually unwise to wake them since they can be excessively disorientated. Far better to lead them safely back to bed. Conversing with a sleep-talker is possible, but often the responses are unintelligible or lack coherence. Sybil Leek relates in *Dreams* that Helen Keller, who was deaf and blind, actually talked in her sleep before she eventually learned to speak in her waking state. The following is an instance of sleep-talking experienced by Mary.

She was sharing a room in college and frequently sat up late reading whilst my room-mate Mary fell asleep. On one occasion, Mary sat straight up in bed and announced in a profound voice: 'I have just discovered the secret of the Universe.' 'Tell me,' I requested. 'Mind your own business,' came the response.

External noises can also have an influence on our dreams. How often has the alarm clock been the culprit, transformed by the dream mind into all manner of monsters, or fire engine or police car sirens? Any crash or bang in the night gets similar treatment, while a snoring partner can be translated into a rumbling earthquake or a snarling animal. And the sound of a screaming vixen has all sorts of potential interpretations. All these possible externals need to be examined when arriving at any form of dream interpretation. For example, I once fell asleep with the radio on and dreamt that my husband was swinging the door to and fro, trying to encourage my daughter to enter. I was worried. Then I was near a serving hatch that did not shut properly and a mangy tiger jumped through it to grab some chewed bones near me. I woke thinking I must keep the doors closed. I then heard the radio, which had been on in the background for some time, summarizing the news headlines, one of which announced the death of the entertainer Larry Grayson, whose catch phrase had been 'Shut that door!'. Hearing the repeated headline from the radio, my subconscious had picked it up and made its own interpretation.

Some noises can be internal rather than external, manifesting as an explosion or a shot inside the head, or occasionally as a brilliant white light. These are physical in origin and are believed to originate from a build-up of static electricity stimulating the occipital area of the brain. However, they can still be absorbed into a dream.

Sleep Disturbance

Some of the factors contributing to sleep disturbance may also affect our periods of dreaming. Many of them are avoidable. For example, watching frightening or stimulating late-night television programmes, having extreme arguments, or experiencing any particularly distressing situation at night will naturally excite brain activity. Many forms of food and drink also have a reputation for disturbing sleep, including cheese, coffee, spicy food or a large meal late at night. However, the supposed effects of large meals are entirely subjective, with little proven truth, except that the stomach obviously needs to rest too.

Abuse of alcohol, however, is a most common cause of sleep disturbance. It leads to very deep sleep for the first 90 minutes or so, but the following period of REM sleep can hardly manifest as the speeding up of the brainwaves, which helps us surface from deep sleep, is extremely sluggish. Instead, the sleeper remains mostly in the deep Delta state. The next phase is one of extreme wakefulness followed by a period of deep and fitful sleep and a reluctance to wake up in the morning. This means that the normal dream process has not been able to function correctly, which could account for the symptoms of hangover and/or addiction. Alcoholics tend to have frightening nightmares, often involving ferocious animals. They also tend to remember their dreams in remarkable detail and the subject matter can intrude into their waking time, producing phobias, hallucinations or paranoia.

Drugs can also upset sleep, with quite a few inhibiting the natural REM patterns. These can include prolonged prescribed medication, such as asthma relief, heart pills and digestion palliatives, as well as recreational drugs. People who take drugs can remain in the very deep Delta levels and their dream patterns can become disturbed. Weaning oneself off drugs can cause an increase in nightmares and anxiety dreams. Short-term medication can also have a temporarily disruptive effect on REM sleep.

Astral Travel

Our dream life may also be affected by the phenomenon of astral travel. The experience of an increasing number of people has led to the belief that a part of us, known as the astral body, actually leaves the physical body when we fall asleep. The astral body can travel vast distances, and it is perhaps while we are in this state that we experience our flying dreams. Those who can 'see' the astral body agree that it closely resembles the physical body and is connected to the sleeping body by a 'silver cord'.

There are several factors which give credence to this theory and there are now many recorded examples of OBEs (out-of-body experiences), particularly in relation to near-death experiences. So many people have described being out of their bodies, of having no physical sensations but being able to hear and observe, that there is now clear evidence for the existence of a level of consciousness which is quite separate from our physical condition. I, myself, have had such an experience. I was aware of sitting on top of a wardrobe – which was, in fact, impossible, since there was insufficient room – and looking down on the sleeping forms of myself and my two room-mates. The moment was brief but extremely clear.

Sudden awakenings or disturbances cause the astral to return to the sleeping body at great speed. This gives rise, in the dream state, to a sensation of falling or crashing, often resulting in a nasty ending to the dream. Sometimes there is a misalignment causing that ghastly 'out-of-sorts' sensation on awakening, often accompanied by headaches, nausea or general grogginess. The best cure is to turn over and go back to sleep so as to become re-aligned, but so rarely can we indulge ourselves in this way that we often have to endure several hours of discomfort before we thoroughly feel 'ourselves' again.

Where does the astral body go each night? There are many theories. The main one is that each of us needs to review our waking life by taking an overview of it. This occurs during the dream period, when 'rising above things' in this manner allows us not only to see the whole day, but also our whole lives, which would explain why we can sometimes see into the future. It is rather like being on top of a tall building or monument in any busy city. When we are down at street level we are mostly conscious of the crowded pavements and the seething traffic. If we climb a little way up, however, we can see much further afield. From the top we are able to look over a wide distance, and see all manner of things as traffic and people go about their daily business. We can even see accidents about to happen, but would be unable to do anything to prevent them.

Other theories suggest that we go journeying simply for the fun of it, or for healing or rescue work. There is evidence to show that people have been cured at a distance by a visit from a healer. Other dreamers tell of going on rescue missions, visiting people in great need or dire distress and supporting them through their crises.

So, all in all, the dream state is a very busy condition. While we are asleep our physical body continues to function automatically, but is at the same time affected by dream imagery from the 'sleeping' mind. Dreaming also appears to be essential for our general health and well-being. If we can learn how to interpret, or even influence, our dreams, we will have acquired a valuable tool for self-healing.

2

....

What is Healing?

The Natural Healing Power of the Body

Healing is a spontaneous function of the body which takes place without any apparent conscious participation on our part. When the need arises, the body simply rallies its defences. For example, if we have a bruise, a cut or a broken bone, we bathe, wash or set it, and then leave nature to take its course. And healing takes place. It is what we expect. We do not envisage non-repair.

For the more virulent illnesses – viruses, infections, parasites – we tend to look for outside help. Initially, this can mean looking in the medicine cupboard, but more usually we consult a qualified doctor for support. The number of patients in surgeries and hospitals show how most of us believe in the doctor's capabilities and take the medicines prescribed for us, trusting that they will work. In most cases, our natural defences are then able to increase their effectiveness, speeding up the healing process and returning us to good health.

Most of us have heard someone praise their doctor, saying how just seeing them makes them feel better. In the doctor–patient relationship, the one is dispensing and the other receiving; but there is actually something else taking place to which the patient's psyche responds. Some kind of link occurs on an unconscious level which brings about healing. Animals recognize what is going on immediately and remain very calm in the hands of a healer. In fact some animals will actually seek one out.

Chronic illnesses, such as arthritis, allergies or heart problems, can be genetic in origin but they can also sometimes be an indication that the natural healing processes are either being impeded or have become faulty. Our natural defences are working to the best of their ability but are in need of assistance. With diseases such as cancer, it appears that the defence mechanisms do not even recognize the problem.

The Healing Power of the Mind

In recent years there has been a considerable change in our attitude towards illness. We have moved away from considering illness to be solely a physical problem towards a more holistic approach. We now understand much better that healing is about balance, and that the whole person is involved – body, mind and spirit. If we treat one without the others, we may well be ignoring the very source of the problem.

So when we are ill, how does the mind become involved? Doctors themselves state that 80 per cent of illnesses are psychosomatic – self-induced. This is where we need to be very honest with ourselves. Do we have any hidden agendas? By that I mean, what do we secretly gain from being ill?

Frequently illness is a cry for help, or an indication that we need a change in attitude. A simple example of this is when we hate our jobs or find our work environment unpleasant, even intolerable, and get the 'Monday morning feeling' – a nebulous, depressing, under-the-weather feeling which is there when we wake and can persist well into the day. We are not really ill, but we can talk ourselves into staying at home and retiring to bed. Similar types of dis-ease with mild, unidentifiable symptoms can occur whenever we have to do anything that we don't like, that frightens us or makes us feel pressured. The problem with this is that slowly but surely it can develop into something more identifiable.

It is important to be honest and think about how we present ourselves to the world. For instance, I have a periodic back problem and sometimes find myself getting out of my car as if I were experiencing an extreme spasm, even when I've not had a bad pain for weeks. Why the exhibition? Why do I want everyone to see my pain? My hidden agenda, or my secondary gain, is that I want attention, even from a distance, and any kind of attention will do. It is the classic 'poor little old me' syndrome, or PLOMS disease as a friend of mine calls it.

If we are really honest with ourselves, many of us suffer from various ailments, some very severe, whose secondary gain is the attention we crave. If this is the case, it is important to realize that by simply 'curing' our physical symptoms we are not necessarily doing ourselves a favour. If a cure should take place without our having understood the underlying cause of the problem, it may not be long before we develop a fresh set of symptoms. Listen carefully to the language of those with chronic illnesses – many of them are self-effacing, even self-sacrificing, classic cases of PLOMS. We need to ask ourselves whether we too are playing the secondary gain game.

In the main, very busy people are seldom ill, even when exposed to massive infection. Look at most local doctors. They are subject to major exposure to illness in surgeries and hospitals – both hotbeds of disease. In fact any of us in direct contact with the public is equally vulnerable to infection. So why is it that some people never seem to get ill?

One of the greatest defences in our immune system is the expectation that we will enjoy good health. Although healing is essentially a spontaneous process which can be assisted by medical intervention, it is also greatly influenced by the mind. It seems we are what we think: if we expect to recover, healing seems to be accelerated. It is also a well-known fact that sick people with the 'right' attitude improve more quickly than those without. There is a tendency, however, to opt out of the healing process, to be passive and expect the doctor to wave a magic wand. Once we accept that we can take part in our own healing process, miracles can happen.

Healing our Lives

We can begin to help ourselves by examining our lifestyle, for there is little value in expecting pristine health while at the same time over-indulging ourselves. This does not mean taking on a stringent regime, but rather acting with moderation. Nutrition is important, so cutting down on the foods that we don't need and increasing our intake of those that we do can only be beneficial. Smoking, drinking alcohol and taking recreational drugs can all impede our body's effectiveness, so decisions have to be made. Similarly, endless pill-popping of any sort, that is neither essential nor prescribed, should be examined. When we begin to realize that most of these indulgences come under the heading of 'dependencies', we can direct our attention to our hidden agendas and from there to the deeper emotions which generate this behaviour. Dreams are one of the best ways of discovering our hidden depths.

Stress can play a major role in undermining our health, and yet today we can rarely avoid it. Regrettably, stress has almost become fashionable. If we are not out there overdoing everything, there must be something wrong with us – we feel we are failures, drop-outs or oddities. We have become victims of the belief that we must keep up with, or be better than, our peers. And, with our systems on constant alert, our bodies suffer from all kinds of tensions and emotions. In the end something has to give and we become sick. We need to ask if any secondary gain is worth pushing ourselves to such limits.

Sometimes we find ourselves in situations where we feel trapped and unable to change things. Worst of all, there often seems to be no solution. Such impasses are common and can frequently lead to illness and depression. In such situations it is as though there are two equal and opposing forces confronting each other and the result is stalemate. This is what often occurs in the majority of relationships and interchanges between human beings, where we expect the 'opposing force' to change, and to mould themselves into a person with whom we are comfortable. At the same time, however, we see no reason why we should change ourselves. What we fail to acknowledge is that, within certain civilized parameters, everyone is entitled to behave as they want.

Looking at the impasse again, we can perhaps realize that the ability to change ourselves is a sign of strength, not weakness. Even the smallest change will cause the 'opposing force' to alter its position. The situation will no longer be the same, and herein lies the strength of being able to change. Furthermore, to change ourselves is to heal ourselves.

The Healing Power of Illness

It may seem a strange thing to say, but illness can itself sometimes be part of the healing process. In fact, it is becoming increasingly acknowledged that being ill can be an important learning exercise on our path to health and well-being. Let me give you an example.

A dance teacher developed a disease which prevented her from dancing any more. She became very depressed and wanted help and support from her mother. However, she found she could not really tell her mother her true feelings and she became angry with her mother and herself about this barrier. Talking with her revealed that she had always been able to express her emotions best through music and dance. On stage she was immensely expressive, so we suggested she find some music which mirrored her present feelings and, even with her limited movement, use it to exorcize her repressed feelings. The same conversation revealed that, when it came to strong feelings, the dancer was unable to express herself vocally. She had been using her dance instead of her voice to avoid the ugliness of confrontation. With this realization, she managed to open a dialogue with her mother that previously would have been impossible and her condition slowly improved. Without her illness, this discovery might never have been made and the healing might not have happened.

Self-healing

Perhaps the best way to describe healing is to say that an exchange of energy takes place, with the healer amplifying the process. In self-healing it is the mind correctly focusing on the need which causes the amplification of the healing energies.

Self-healing can take the form of prayers, visualizations, self-hypnosis, dreamwork, or a simple implicit belief that a cure is possible. It is also helpful to plug into an appropriate healing source which can be drawn from a particular belief system – God, Jesus, Mary, Allah, Muhammad, the healing spirit, the Goddess, the creative source, to name but a few possibilities. When initiating the self-healing process, it is important to concentrate on a healthy body, or on the body returning to health, and not on the illness. It is easy to forget this and focus on the problem instead, which may inadvertently amplify the illness.

In self-healing it is also important to understand that somewhere inside each of us there is, to use computer language, the program which created us when we were in the womb and enabled us to grow into adults. This was not a conscious process; it simply happened without our interference. This reinforces the premise that the body can work on its own. Thus, by instilling the need for healing into the deeper levels of our minds, we should be able to tap into this program, making self-healing possible.

3

The Development of Dream Healing

D reams and their interpretations have been recorded since the beginning of time. One very early dream is that of Thotmes IV from around 1420 BC. It is recorded on a sheet of granite between the paws of the Great Sphinx. At that time the Sphinx was neglected and beginning to disappear under the sand. Thotmes dreamt that he would be ruler of Egypt and have a long and prosperous reign. On awakening he saw the Great Sphinx in its sorry state and vowed to keep it beautiful for the rest of his life. Many other hieroglyphic texts on dream interpretation have been discovered, for the Egyptians were great believers in the power of dreams and oracles, and had temples dedicated to dream healing (*see* page 30).

The value of dreaming is also mentioned in the Hindu Vedas and Upanishads, dating from 800 BC, while the Sumarians together with the Assyrians and the Babylonians all recognized An Za Qar, their god of dreams. The dream of Gilgamesh, King of Sumaria, is one of the most famous early ones recorded on tablets dating from around 650 BC. He was regularly troubled by dreams which his mother, the goddess Ninsun, interpreted for him. Gilgamesh was warned in a dream of the death of his friend Enkidu.

In the very early records of China and Japan, there is the often quoted instance of the Sage, Chuang-tzu. He dreamed he was a butterfly, conscious only of following his instincts as a butterfly. Suddenly he woke up and realized that he was a human being. He was then unsure whether he was a man dreaming he was a butterfly or whether he was a butterfly dreaming it was a man.

Dream Traditions Around the World

The story of Chuang-tzu touches on a question that has troubled many great thinkers down the centuries – what is the dividing line between waking and dreaming? As this question relates directly to the understanding of our own dreams, there is much we can learn from those cultures for whom no such division exists.

For the native Australians the whole of life evolved in the Dreamtime, or *altjeringa*, *tjukurapa* or the *Bamun* depending on tribal origins. Aborigines consider that we dream everything around us and that we relate and interweave with it. Ordinary everyday events, and especially the natural world that most of us would consider commonplace, are imbued with supernatural forces.

Their creation myth states that all time exists simultaneously. There is no past, present or future. It is all in the now. They live in a magical place of the permanent no-where, no-when of the myth. Thus native Australians consider themselves at all times to be dreaming the dream. Many tribes totally rely on what their dreams foretell. They possess such vivid imagination and inward intensity that at times it is impossible for them to differentiate between the waking and dreaming state.

An example of their beliefs is their ability to traverse vast inhospitable country. Members of the tribe dream their totem animal, say a kangaroo, and then see it manifested in the surrounding terrain, either as an actual animal or as an outline in trees, rock formations or other natural phenomena. These then act as perfectly reliable signposts.

A similar viewpoint is held by the Bushmen of the Kalahari. In *The Heart of the Hunter*, Laurens van der Post tells of how, when pressed to explain their creation myths in comparison with those of the Christian, the Bushmen find it difficult since they consider that their whole life is a dream and they are being 'dreamed' by it. So where does the dream begin and end? Where lies reality?

Many African societies set great store by dreams, believing that they are linked to their destiny. They have a deep belief in ancestor worship, and think that wisdom can be accessed through making contact with the spirits of the past. Dreams are a natural source for such communication. They believe that their ancestors care for them and through dreams will inform them of important future events, both pleasures and disasters, which naturally enables sensible preparations to be made. Records show that there have been successful cures for sickness from dream messages. Even political decisions are made from time to time based on dream advice. This can, of course, be a two-edged sword, with negative actions resulting. Sometimes they are convinced that nightmares are actually sent to them deliberately, and that people can use dreams to wish evil or even death on them.

Dr Roderick Peters, a medical doctor who practised in West Africa, states that patients frequently described their dreams when they came to consult him. It was apparent that they felt there was a distinct link between the dream state and their ill- nesses. It was fairly commonplace for the local witch doctors to put spells on people, which patients thought the Western doc- tor could remove. However, Dr Peters quotes a case where he could do nothing to help, and a perfectly healthy individual died within eight days with no symptoms whatsoever of any physical disease.

The *Tibetan Book of the Dead* describes dreaming as the intermediate stage between life and death – a form of prepara- tion for the eventual transition. When we fall asleep we enter the *bardo* of becoming, a dream world. We become a part of it and participate in dream experiences, which have their own reality that disguises the fact that we are dreaming.

Dreams were important to the Tibetans who felt that they were vital to their spiritual growth. If a dream seemed particu- larly significant or worrying they would visit the priest at the local monastery for an interpretation. They firmly believed that a part of them, rather like a double, left the body in the dream state and went travelling. In Tibetan medicine these out-of-body states are always examined as being of significance.

Denise Linn quotes a Tibetan method of dream recall where you imagine a glowing blue sphere in the throat area in which you place your desire to remember and hold the image while falling asleep. She goes on to say that research has shown that the back of the throat controls dream activity and focusing on this area as we fall asleep stimulates our dreams.

Linn also gives very clear accounts of the Native American use of dreams, particularly among the Iroquois. She describes how people would travel great distances to act out ritual dream dramas. There was an annual festival called the Onoharoia, where dreams would be acted out theatrically. This was known as the *Ondinnonk*. The Native Americans felt that this was of crucial importance and that failure to acknowledge the messages of dreams could bring dire results.

Certain tribes believed in the Great Dream which ruled each person's life. They maintained that each person had one dream, dreamed in the womb and forgotten at birth. Positive characteristics such as courage, creativity, wisdom and consideration for others were considered to be talents bestowed in this Great Dream. Children were encouraged to remember and explore their dreams from the youngest age and young men would fast until they had visions of their 'song of life'.

Originally, dream-catching was part of the initiation ceremonies of certain tribes. The initiate had to learn this art, making a magical circle around himself and then incubating his visions and dreams. The idea was to capture the messages from the spirits in the element of air enclosed within his circle. The dream-catcher is the physical expression of this particular rite.

Like many other cultures, Native Americans felt it difficult to define the border between the waking and dream state. Lucid dreaming – a dream state in which the dreamer is able to control the outcome of the dream – was common and dream incubation the norm to assist with healing, hunting and fertility. They were also known to amplify dreams to bring about healing. There is an example from the 1600s in the Onondaga country of a sick girl being persuaded by the medicine man that she had dreamed of nine feasts. If she were to have these feasts she would be cured.

Sometimes a particular person or animal would appear regularly in dreams, bringing help and advice and generally giving the dreamer a sense of warmth and great security. These dream guides were common, and were treated like friends and counsellors, to be consulted at any time, day or night.

The Senoi people of Malaysia are frequently quoted in literature about dreams because they live their lives from a dream perspective. Each day dreams are shared either within the family or within the tribe. Interpretation is a joint enterprise. Solutions are offered for difficult dreams and appropriate actions taken to improve the dreamer's life and attitudes. Good dreams are praised and precognitive ones acknowledged with suitable preparations for the foretold event.

Dangers in dreams have to be confronted, and pleasure on whatever level participated in. A clear ending to each dream needs to be achieved. Death is acknowledged as an end and therefore needs to be experienced in dreams. Dream sex and dream lovers are acknowledged and enjoyed. Often help is provided by dream guides. As a result of these practices, the Senoi people are psychologically healthy.

Shamanism was and still is practised among many cultures around the world and the training of the shaman is deeply connected with altered states of consciousness and frequently involves dreaming. It is usually a difficult and painful route requiring great dedication. The would-be shaman firstly needs to learn absolute discipline of mind and body. He needs complete control of thought and the power of thought. Then follows the initiation of ritual death and rebirth which takes place in an altered or dream state. In many cultures this is drug-induced; however, it is much more powerful in the dream or meditative state since the brain is not impaired or influenced by external stimulation. The novice learns to make contact with both his and the collective unconscious through a route that he can command at any moment without assistance.

Having used the dream state for his initiation, the shaman continues to employ it for the benefit of those around him. For dream healing, he uses the incubation methods similar to those used in the ancient dream temples. Guided by the shaman the patient, after elaborate purifying rites, seeds his dream with a request for the correct treatment to cure him.

Dream Healing Temples

The tradition of dream temples goes back at least as far as the Egyptians who had dream temples where priests and priestesses took the major questions of the day and incubated or 'seeded' them into the dream state of visionaries – a process whereby a question is implanted into the mind immediately prior to falling asleep and one awakens with the answer. Egyptian records also reveal that dream healing in temples was a popular and important process, and sick people would sleep in the temples in the belief that they would be visited by the god of healing, Imhotep (known as Asclepius to the later Greeks and Romans). The request for a cure was seeded into the dream with the help of the priests who would then assist with interpretation.

The Greeks and Romans continued the tradition of healing temples, which they dedicated to Asclepius, who was supposed to have been tutored in healing by the deities Chiron and Athene. Healing temples spread throughout the ancient world. At one time there were over 400 of them, the most famous of which was at Epidaurus, the ruins of which can be seen today. Their common feature was the serpent. In some cases, the sick would even sleep among snakes to help effect a cure. This symbol became more familiar as the caduceus – two serpents entwining the staff of healing – and is still seen today in the badges of many healing professions (such as the British Medical Association).

Healing temples were also to be found in China, where they took the form of special shrines where meditating supplicants would dream of visions of Kwan Yin, their healing *bohdisattva*. Buddhist and Shinto temples in Japan had dream oracles for healing. Certain rituals had to be performed to purify the sick person to a state where he could receive guidance and a vision of the ruling deity. The most famous Shinto shrine was at Usa in Kyushi, and was dedicated to the god, Hachiman.

The Modern Perspective

Freud

It is really to Sigmund Freud (1865–1939) that we owe our current interest in dreams. It is because of his work that we no longer allow dreams to be ignored in our understanding of the personality. According to Freud, the desire for life is our prime motivation, and therefore we are driven by our procreative instincts – that is, sex. He felt that many of our unconscious restraints develop in childhood, through guilt and conflict with authority, and are therefore frequently of long standing. He suggested that during sleep our internal censor has less energy and allows repressed desires to surface – the wish-fulfilment dream. Our dreams thus reveal a part of us that cannot be easily accessed in any other way.

To explore this theory Freud encouraged his patients to talk about their dreams and any thoughts that they provoked, thus developing a chain of thoughts, later known as the 'free association of ideas'. However, because of his rigid views on the procreation urge, Freud fell victim to the 'experimenter effect'. This is a danger for all dream interpreters – the tendency to impose their dogma on others, seeing only what they want to see. Research has shown that the beliefs, feelings and inclinations of the interpreter can be the deciding factors as to the outcome. Thus, if the interpreter has a preconceived idea about a dreamer's problem, he can easily make the mistake of seeing the dream symbols only in that limited context.

Cayce

Edgar Cayce (1877–1945) saw dreams as being of great significance. He believed them to be our sixth sense, and stated that we tune into higher levels in dreams and become aware of what is being built and what may be projected into the physical in the future. In fact our whole future is built in this way, which can give credence to precognitive dreams – dreams about future events, a knowing in advance.

Known as the Sleeping Prophet, Cayce was able to help people in many ways whilst in an altered state of consciousness, similar to the dream state. People came to him with problems – physical, mental or spiritual – and often received profound and thought-provoking answers. He was able to diagnose and heal in this state and it was not necessary for the patient be with him or even in the same house. Distance was irrelevant.

Jung

The greatest influence on modern dream interpretation has probably been the work of Carl Gustav Jung (1875–1961). In the early part of his career, Jung allied himself with Freud's analytical psychoanalytical work, and Freud thought of him as his 'Crown Prince'. The association ended around 1916, when a book published by Jung came to Freud's attention which described sexual symbolism as part of a broader symbolizing function, and the sexual energy called libido as part of a more general, innate energy in human beings.

Moreover, Jung portrayed the 'id' – Freud's name for a concept of the primitive psyche where repressed material was stored – as an unconscious layer of the psyche which mediated to consciousness *not only* repressed material but also universal and archetypal patterns. Put more simply, archetypes are images, things or symbols that emerge from the collective unconscious, to which we react without conscious thought.

Jung created a list of 12 major personalities which could manifest in the dream state (*see* pages 77–85). He also developed the idea of the masculine and feminine aspects, known respectively as the animus and anima, as being present within the human psyche. Ideally these should be well-balanced but frequently there is an over-dominance in one direction or the other to the detriment of normal functioning for the individual. Alongside these he explored the ego and its shadow.

It was Jung who described us as living in a beautiful house, the mansion of the soul, but rarely leaving the basement. This is because in dreams the house represents the self, with each part having a different significance, as will be explained later (*see* Chapter 11). He was able to apply this imagery to the human situation. For example, we might put in the foundations and start to build but never finish, or there might be rooms which we never use or even visit.

According to Jung, dreams not only provide a key to current problems; they also advise us how to develop our full human potential. What is important, however, is to interpret the dream with all its many various and symbolic meanings before applying it to the dreamer's situation. Failing to do so can incorrectly colour the result. In Jung's words, we should constantly be asking what the dream is saying.

4

The Bizarre World of Dreams

D reams fall into various categories which need to be identified in the course of interpretation. For healing purposes we must be clear what these are, otherwise we may be misinforming ourselves and searching for meanings which are not there. Thus the type of dream needs to be our first consideration. This chapter identifies and describes the main categories.

Literal Dreams

The most common type of dream is the literal dream – a sort of daily review. These tend to be logical and excessively normal, and are the product of our intellect rather than our intuition. They reflect the outside world like a photograph rather than a creative composition. They are often an action replay of the day's events, and give us the opportunity to review and find other ways of doing things.

Wish-fulfilment Dreams

As mentioned earlier, wish-fulfilment dreams were the basis of much of the work of Sigmund Freud, although today we no longer set so much store by them. They are remarkably common and do not carry great depths of meaning. Examples of these are being with a lover or ex-lover, winning large sums of money, holidaying in some tropical place and being famous. In many ways they are an extension of daydreaming. We must be careful, however, not to dismiss them since there is just a chance that they are trying to communicate something of greater significance. If they keep recurring, we should then ask ourselves why we need to live outside reality, or whether our mind is trying to tell us something about the choices we are making.

Compensatory Dreams

This is a strange category of dreaming which closely resembles wish-fulfilment. It was discovered that people in concentration camps rarely had bad dreams or any sort of nightmare. Their dream worlds were full of magic, beauty and pleasant environments, and peopled by healthy and happy individuals. The theory is that these dreams compensated for their appalling experiences in their waking hours.

This can also happen in reverse. For example, a woman who had everything she could want in life kept having frightening recurring dreams about the death of her son and husband in some dreadful ordeal. No amount of ordinary interpretation came up with any solution and it was felt that she had tapped into the collective unconscious for these dreams to compensate for her guilt about her rich lifestyle. These could also have been far memory dreams (*see* page 39).

Daydreams and Reveries

Daydreaming and reveries are incredibly creative states. We daydream when our minds wander during our waking hours. It is a strange state in which it is often difficult to say whether we are awake or asleep. We are completely absorbed in a fantasy world which can be extremely emotive and productive. It is a clear altered state of consciousness. This highly relaxed state allows the mind to unravel problems and permits flashes of inspiration to come to the surface.

The classic example of positive results of daydreaming is that of Archimedes who, while dozing in his bath, suddenly understood the principle of buoyancy. He is said to have leapt out and run naked through the streets shouting '*Eureka!*' – 'I have found it!'

Thomas Edison, the inventor, believed so strongly in the semi-conscious state that he kept a couch in his laboratory on which to relax and dream. He actually held a small brass ball in his hand to prevent his falling asleep. If his hand relaxed in sleep, the ball fell onto a metal plate and woke him. The results of his dreaming included the phonograph and the incandescent lamp.

Hypnogogic and Hypnopompic States

Earlier we mentioned hypnogogic and hypnopompic images which occur in that period between sleeping and waking – the world of surrealism. Examination of the works of great surrealist artists gives us some understanding of these images. Salvador Dali truly captures the weirdness of the hypnogogic with his strange treatment of everyday objects. A further example is the obscure humour of the cartoons of *Monty Python*. Both are characterized by a feeling of obsession and extremes.

However, these need not always be weird and require careful observation since they may be responses to an incubation request. One night as I was dropping off I saw myself choosing a tree to plant in my secret garden (*see* page 134) – actually a windswept clifftop. I was choosing something appropriate like a windswept thorn bush, when this was snatched away and replaced by an enormous bare-branched ash tree, like changing the slide in a projector. It gave me quite a shock. This had an important meaning for me. The ash tree is often considered to be the 'tree of life'.

False Awakening

This is an interesting condition where we are asleep and dreaming but think that we are awake. For example, a woman dreamed that she was getting up in the morning, going through the whole routine of dressing, eating and leaving for work, only to wake up and find that none of this had actually happened. False awakening may also occur when napping. We believe we have woken and are continuing with our day, often achieving quite important feats, only to awake and find we haven't even started. This is the stage that often immediately precedes lucid dreaming and when recognized can be used to take us into this state.

Precognitive Dreams and Premonitions

How is it possible to see into the future? As yet, there are no conclusive answers. Chapter 1 touched on one possibility, that of astral travelling or being out of one's body. Precognition is knowing about something in advance; a premonition is a warning in advance, a foreboding, without necessarily knowing exactly what is going to happen.

As a young corporal on the Somme, Adolf Hitler had a nightmare in which he was being suffocated by falling earth and debris. On waking, the dream was so vivid that he felt unable to breathe so he ran outside. Within minutes a shell landed on the bunker and killed all the occupants. This is a clear instance of a dream changing the face of history.

Precognitive dreams about major disasters are well-documented. Before the Aberfan disaster, many people dreamed of the moving slurry hill and the enveloped schoolyard. My own grandmother dreamed of the 1906 San Francisco earthquake. The Agadir earthquake was similarly foreseen by many dreamers. Other disasters such as the sinking of the *Titanic*, assassinations of presidents and prime ministers, and railway or aeroplane crashes have been foretold in dreams.

Another strange aspect of precognitive dreaming is knowing details and facts that should be completely beyond our ken. An exponent of this type of dreaming is Chris Robinson, who currently helps the police with solving crimes. On one occasion he dreamed of a high fence linked with a disaster. On waking, he remembered that this fence surrounded a military establishment and knew the dream was about a bomb. He warned the necessary authorities, who naturally thought he was mad or had planted the bomb himself. However, he was proved right. He has had other dreams where he has found lost people and dead bodies and is now taken seriously by the police.

George Cranley used to dream of race winners on a regular basis, and thus made sufficient funds to bring himself and a colleague to Britain from South Africa. Another young man, who had been considering suicide having lost all his money on horses and being unable to honour his debts, was saved by a friend dreaming of a winning horse.

Premonitions are a clear warning about some future danger, which, of course, we are quite at liberty to ignore. Our dreams give us the option to change those things that we can change and to prepare for those we can't. If a death dream is truly about someone's death, then when it happens in reality, we have already had the opportunity to get over the shock and the experience is easier to handle. For this reason it makes us of more use to others and we can be a real support to them in their time of crisis.

Examples of this are dreams – usually during times of war or extreme stress – in which women have seen their sons, boyfriends or husbands standing in the room with them. Subsequent investigations have usually proved that this experience coincided with the moment of death.

Far Memory Dreams and *Déjà Vu*

Far memory dreams are dreams of past lives, of having lived before in a different period. We may find ourselves of a different gender and age. These dreams can be identified by their clarity and general simplicity. Although not very common, they tend to create strong and lasting impressions.

How can we tell the dream is about a past life? The answer is that we can't. Whilst acknowledging that a very few people might never have had any knowledge of the subject matter of such a dream, most of us are likely to have had some prior exposure at some time or another, however slight, through books, television, and so on. It is sensible, therefore, to search the memory for such prior information before getting too excited. Again we do not know what prompts such dreams, unless we have been specifically exploring past life recall. There is a theory that some illnesses are carried on from previous lives, which is why they don't respond to treatment. Far memory dreams then are guides to understanding this. Again, with this extra knowledge we can incubate for answers.

My own brief experience of far memory dreaming occurred quite a few years ago. I dreamed I was a priest in some kind of temple with two other people, one of whom was my helper and the other the patient. There was a stone couch. I knew we had to lie on the couch with the patient between us. The helper's job was to protect all of us psychically. We had to go to sleep and I would then meet the patient in the dream state and heal him. At the time I knew absolutely nothing about Asclepius and his healing dream temples and was quite taken aback when informed. It is ironic but it has only just struck me that my current work is healing through dreams!

Déjà vu is a waking experience where we feel we have seen or experienced a situation on a previous occasion. It is frequently equated with having dreamed but not consciously remembered something. In a healing environment, instances of *déjà vu* can be prompts to act on unacknowledged information received in the dream state. There can, however, be other explanations such as a forgotten early memory or a past life experience. Recording our dreams helps to identify some of the possibilities.

There are several documented cases of children confidently leading adults around venues which none of them had ever visited before. Did they have a precognitive dream or is it a far memory?

Problem-solving and Creative Dreams

It is often said that the best way of dealing with a problem is to 'sleep on it'. When we sleep, the mind is unfettered by waking emotions which colour and obscure solutions. Professor Freidrich Kekulé von Stradonitz, a German chemist, was desperate to discover the molecular structure of a particular chemical. He received the answer in a dream as he was dozing by the fire. He saw repeated visions of a snake eating its tail, and recognized this symbol as being the answer to his difficulty. Thus the knowledge of the benzene ring, on which all combustion engines are based, came into being. It is he that we have to thank for the motor car.

What is interesting here is that he experienced repeated visions. The answer had obviously been available on a number of occasions but his waking mind had not registered the fact. Most of our answers are around us. It is crucial to listen to the 'still, small voice' but not to be governed by it. Learn discrimination.

Albert Einstein acknowledged that his theory of relativity was the result of a childhood dream in which he was speeding downhill on a sledge, going so fast that he was approaching the speed of light. This speed created visual distortions so that when he looked at the sky, the stars and planets were transformed with many different patterns and colours. He is said to have based all of his later work on this dream.

Many great writers, poets, artists and musicians gain their creative inspiration from the dream state. Robert Louis Stevenson is a case in point. Complete stories came to him this way, such as *Dr Jekyll and Mr Hyde* and *Treasure Island*. Before he went to sleep, Stevenson also used to tell himself stories which were then developed in the dream state – a clear example of incubation.

Lewis Carroll's *Alice in Wonderland* is clearly the result of the author's dreaming. In this instance many of the images are markedly archetypal and symbolic. Alice's trip through the looking glass is a classic example of moving into the dream world.

Composers such as Beethoven, Schumann, Mozart and Ravel are said to have been inspired by their dreams and actually heard bits of music which they were able to recall on waking. Guiseppe Tartini wrote 'The Devil's Sonata' following an incredibly vivid dream about Satan playing his violin.

History shows us that there have been many visionaries who have tuned into the dream world. Over 500 years ago, Leonardo da Vinci designed an aeroplane and a submarine. The work of some modern science fiction writers is dream-inspired and may well become reality at some point in the future.

Serial Dreams

These dreams are not so common. They take on the form of a soap opera and each night produces a new instalment. Some dreamers simply cannot wait to get to bed to find out what happens next. Sometimes several sequences occur in the same night with waking periods in between. These serials can last one night or continue over several months and historically have resulted in some great novels being written. We can also develop our healing requests in this way by creating characters and a story around them.

Graham Greene used this serial form of dreaming for inspiration, often waking several times during the night to continue the storyline and develop the plot of his novels. He kept a dream journal which he used to develop his ideas. He would re-read what he had written during the day before going bed and the next part of the story would then unfold in his dreams.

Nightmares and Recurring Dreams

Nightmares result from two sources. Firstly, as mentioned earlier, they can be the brain's interpretation of an actual physical state, such as sleep paralysis, myoclonic jerks, external noises or sudden awakenings. Secondly, they can be brought on by the suppression of all the doubts and fears we are unable to face up to during the day. Dreams of falling and being chased are very common.

Many frightening images are drawn from our own experience and from collective experience portrayed around us in art, literature and the media. If we look at paintings by the early religious artists showing their interpretations of hell and demons, it is hardly surprising that we use these creatures to scare ourselves. And films such as *Psycho* and *Frankenstein* further augment our source of material for nightmares. Combine this with the constant onslaught of images from television, radio and our general environment and the horrors are endless.

Again we need to look back to past experiences to discover why our unconscious minds have chosen certain images. All the monsters, bogeymen and threatening people represent those around us, whether at work, among our social circle or at home. These need to be confronted and dealt with, which often takes courage. Until they are, the nightmares will keep coming. Nightmares indicate that we are not dealing with our problems in life; and if we do not do so, they recur.

Sometimes it is difficult to recognize that our waking circumstances are connected with those of the dream, because different people and places may be involved. The dream mind, however, recognizes the scenario and plays it back to enable us to become more aware so that we can extricate ourselves and stop making the same mistakes. This is what recurring dreams, not necessarily nightmares, are all about. They will repeat and repeat each time we fall into the same traps.

Nightmares, however, have also produced surprising results. James Watt, a Scottish inventor and engineer, had a nightmare in which he was walking through a rain storm of heavy lead pellets rather like hail stones. This led him to realize that if molten lead is dropped from a great height it forms spheres. Thus ball-bearings were discovered.

Another well-documented nightmare is that of Elias Howe

who invented the sewing machine. He was having trouble creating the locking stitch, and dreamed he had been chased by natives who all carried spears which had holes through the blades. He realized that this was the ideal position for the eye of the needle and went on to produce the machine needles we know today.

Flying and Falling Dreams

These are two common types of dream. Flying usually indicates a need to rise above a situation, to take an overview. It can also indicate lucid dreaming (*see* below). Dreamers find themselves flapping as though they had wings, jumping in the air, sailing across the countryside or just simply weightless, with a 'bird's eye view'. The sensation of flying can also be a partial consciousness of astral travelling. Many dreamers really enjoy this freedom and are reluctant to return to the weight of their bodies. During a flying dream we often see our bodies from a great height and can be given clues about our state of health. Alternatively, we might fly to the source of a cure or treatment so that on waking, we know exactly what to do.

Falling, on the other hand, is thought to be an awareness of moving from the waking state to the sleeping one. We use such expressions as 'falling asleep' or 'dropping off'. The return of the astral body to the physical often surfaces in the dream as a fall. On the other hand, the dreamer could be 'heading for a fall', 'falling from grace' or 'falling in love' – just to give a few ideas. Alternatively in a health context we might 'fall for a cold', 'fall pregnant', 'fall under' or 'fall for a disease'.

Lucid Dreaming

Lucid dreaming is a strange category of dreaming which has been the subject of extensive research. It is the state of being asleep and dreaming while actually being aware within the dream state of being asleep and dreaming.

My son once told me of a dream where he was walking on a beach, freshly washed smooth by the receding tide, when he came across some strange signs scored on the sand. While he was looking at them, he became aware that he was in the dream state and that he had to memorize these inscriptions and tell me about them when he awoke. As he described his dream to me, he drew what he had seen. They were runic symbols that suggested that there would be trouble with a partnership. This turned out to be true for me at work.

Through this awareness, it is possible to control and direct the sequence of events in the dream. In other words, you can change the outcome. This is particularly valuable in the case of nightmares or anything that is mildly threatening. Dr Stephen LeBerge of Stanford University, who has researched lucid dreaming, describes it as resembling a laboratory or play-ground in which we can try out new ways of behaving.

Lucid dreaming introduces us to that part of ourselves which creates our dreams. This, in turn, allows us to become more conscious in our daily activities and also to create our own futures by exploring all the possible outcomes in the dream state. From time to time this will affect our interactions with other people, so a high ethical standard needs to be observed.

There is another form of lucid dreaming that, to date, is still in the realms of science fiction – but who knows? The idea is that a trained lucid dreamer can enter and control the dreams of another. By the use of suggestion, he can influence that person to commit acts alien to his normal behaviour. This theory is the basis of a novel in which someone attempts to enter the dreams of a president and guide him to take evil actions. The president experiences nightmares since these dreams go against his philosophy. This is discovered by a group of dream researchers. The hero's task is to enter the dreams of the villain to prevent his dream manipulations. Eventually he succeeds through turning the villain's projected dreams of death in on himself.

Dream Sharing

The above story is plausible since it is possible for dream sharing to happen. This occurs between people who are very close to each other, either mentally and emotionally, or physically – for example, in the same bed. In this instance both parties participate simultaneously in a similar dream. It is rather like tapping into a local level of the collective unconscious. It is not all that common, but has been recorded in entire communities. In *Your Dreams and What They Mean*, Nerys Dee mentions that the people of whole villages in Corsica can have similar dreams on the same night.

A friend who was having a dispute with her partner dreamed that she was dancing at a disco to the song 'Eleanor Rigby'. Her partner dreamed he was at a Beatles concert, tapping his feet in time to 'Eleanor Rigby'. In other words, they were dancing to the same tune, but not together.

A woman dreamed she was getting married to a long-standing family friend who was very neatly dressed and looked well. On the same night the friend's daughter also dreamed that he was getting married but she did not know to whom. In her dream he was also neatly dressed and looked well. It would seem that the man was entering into some sort of contract or commitment which was important enough to get dressed up for, and his looking well showed it to be beneficial. Both the woman and her friend's daughter might have been aware of this. The woman's closer connection in the dream could mean that the venture was her suggestion originally.

Members of a group, especially one meditating or exploring dreams, may find that a common dream theme will emerge. It is also possible to explore dream telepathy, which was researched by Dr Ullman at the Maimonides Medical Center in Brooklyn. His experiments involved a receiver who went to sleep wired to apparatus which would register REM sleep. When he entered the REM state, a 'sender' in another part of the building chose a picture at random from some sealed envelopes and sent it to the sleeper. They were remarkably successful. This could be developed further to a healer sending healing to a sick person. After all, remember the healing temples?

Diagnostic Healing Dreams

To heal ourselves we can create healing dreams, asking our deep unconscious for answers or diagnoses and treatments. We can seed this need into our minds just before falling asleep, requesting the answer through our dreams. For example, someone suffering from a pain might ask their dream self, 'Where is my pain coming from?' or 'What is the reason for my pain?'.

Shirley was worried about a pain in her chest which at times was very severe. Only gentle breathing into the painful area would relieve it. She was afraid that it could be connected with her heart. However, apart from these few occasions she was in very good health. She seeded the request 'Where is my pain coming from?' into her mind just before sleeping. Her dream was as follows:

I was up in a tree crawling out onto a branch when it snapped and I fell. I was aware that I couldn't breathe and was panicking when I saw in front of me a thin vertical pipe with branches. On one of these branches there was a kind of tap where it joined the main pipe. I turned it on and flames shot out of the end of it like a gas jet.

Shirley remembered that she had indeed fallen out of a tree as a child and had been badly winded with a possible broken rib. She decided to go for an x-ray. This revealed that there was some ossification from the old injury which was now pressing occasionally on a nerve in her spine. This was causing the pain in the front of her chest. Thus the pipes related to her spinal cord and ribs, while turning on the tap caused the flame/pain a distance away from the injury. The dream had led her away from her initial worries about her heart to the real seat of the problem.

Incubated Dreams

These are important since they form the central feature of dream healing. Incubation is the process of sowing an idea in our minds just as we fall asleep – the old-fashioned idea of 'sleeping on a problem'. In the morning we will often have the answer, or it might occur to us later in the day. In the majority of cases, this is completely spontaneous. By taking control of this process, incubating or seeding can be made into one of the most valuable aspects of dreaming. The following is an example of an incubated dream:

I asked my dream self about a friend whom I was worrying about. Out of a fog came a form in chain mail. Part of it had blown away and was swaying in the breeze.

The image is clearly about loss of protection. The chain mail could represent the friend's immune system. It could be that he is vulnerable to viruses or even to personal enemies around him.

Self-hypnosis

This is another form of incubation. Through self-analysis we try to pinpoint the area in our psyche which is demanding attention. Armed with this new knowledge, we can go into a quiet meditative state, implanting post-hypnotic suggestions to seed into our dreams. It is similar to a form of affirmation, constantly planting the idea in our deeper levels. It is a good idea to rein-force this by using the seeding procedure just before sleeping.

People undergoing therapy can experience a spontaneous dream response to counselling. This should be given considerable attention as it indicates that something has been stirred. Counselling can stimulate memories of earlier dreams and give a clue to an experience which, unrecognized, is being repeated.

Self-healing Dreams

Some dreams can actually bring about healing in themselves. Sometimes dream visitors will give some form of treatment. These can be our guides or guardian angels, or actual healers astral travelling.

An example of the latter is the documented case of a well-known archaeologist who was struck down by a virulent fever while in Egypt. He dreamed that he was visited by a doctor, dressed in the conventional black coat and striped trousers of the time, who gave him something for his fever. The dream doctor told the patient that he had come from Britain and was often called upon in the dream state to go healing. The archaeologist subsequently recovered and on his return home appealed via the radio for such a doctor. A GP from Scotland came forward and identified himself as the dream helper. He exactly fitted the dreamed doctor.

The following helper dream was experienced by a woman who was bleeding profusely and was very debilitated. On being sent to a specialist, she was found to have a growth. She was devastated and that night had a dream. These are her words:

My lovely Eastern mother who had died a few years previously was sitting at a table in a well-lit area, which could have been a warehouse. I was sitting opposite her. 'Why are you so sad?' she asked. 'I hurt so much,' I said. At this she leant forward gently, her hand reaching out to my navel. She pulled out a lump the size of an avocado seed. It was bloody and had ugly roots.

She woke the next morning with a throbbing pain and tenderness around the navel. On her next visit to the doctor, he was somewhat bemused to find nothing growing!

5

•••••••••••••••••••••••

Dream Healing (1) – Getting Started

B efore starting to use your dreams for self-healing, there are a couple of important points to remember. Firstly, if you are currently being treated by a doctor, any medication that you have been prescribed should be continued and any advice still followed. Your dreams will work with the tools they are given and according to the current condition of the physical body, medicines and all. Secondly, it is vital to realize that dreaming, unaided, cannot always cure our problems. We need to give it some help through maintaining our bodies, at least at the very basic level of nutrition, elimination, breathing and exercise. None of this need be excessive.

To get any benefit from our dreams we need to be in control. Those who dream regularly can start recording them immediately. For those who have difficulty in remembering dreams, the following procedure should be adopted. As you are falling asleep, tell yourself that you will remember your dream. With a little practice, this will work and you will be ready to start healing yourself.

The Incubated or Seeded Dream Technique

This is the most important dream healing procedure, and it requires very little skill to start it. It is like a hidden releasing-mechanism for creating a better lifestyle through subtly changing ourselves. If you have discovered how to remember your dreams, you are already practising it.

The incubation or seeding method is simple. First decide what you want to know and then think about it positively and clearly before you fall asleep. The next vital step is to remember any dream on waking. To do this, make a deliberate point of sowing the seed and asking for an answer. In the morning, it is vital to give your full attention to discovering any response, because an answer can come in many forms.

The basic method

To use dream incubation to full effect, adopt the following procedure.

- First ask yourself what it is you want to know. Do you want a diagnosis? Do you want to know what treatment you need? Do you want to know the prognosis (the future outcome)?
- Next decide how you will send your dream. Will you use a straightforward request, imagery or affirmations?
- Either write or draw your request, or else focus on it with your mind.
- Tell yourself to remember the dream as you go to sleep.
- Record your dream when you wake up and effect an interpretation.
- Remain alert for any synchronicities that occur during the next day or so.
- If necessary, re-incubate in the next dream session.

When working with incubation absolute clarity is crucial. It often takes us some time to acknowledge the fact that we are unwell. We ignore it or push it to one side until it demands our attention. In many cases we can make the diagnosis easily ourselves – the common cold, for example, or a headache, indigestion, or a tummy upset. From experience, we know the treatment, the time period and probable outcome. It would only be necessary to introduce dream incubation if these common complaints persisted or did not follow the 'normal' course back to full health. It would then become obvious that we did not really know the diagnosis.

What is important is the treatment and the proper action to take. The dream state can identify that because the body knows what it needs. Take, for example, the food cravings of the pregnant mother. If analysed they would probably show a missing vitamin or mineral in the diet. This worked for me during pregnancy when I developed a mad desire for watercress and sardines, both of which have a higher than average calcium content. On another occasion it was cocoa and curry, which contain high levels of iron. These patterns or synchronicities can also show up in dreams. So trust your body and your dream mind.

It can also be valuable to have some idea of how long an illness is going to last. This prevents us from pushing ourselves too hard too soon. We do not return to lifting furniture just after straining our backs or to heavy manual work when a scab has just fallen off a wound on our hands. We give it a day or two to strengthen or harden up. It is the same with any illness, and dream incubation can help to determine the amount of time needed.

Using a straightforward request sometimes needs a little explanation. Clarity is important here as normally we are very woolly-thinking. The question should be simple and require a simple answer. For example, just asking what is the matter could refer to a number of problems, not necessarily illness. The response would, therefore, be somewhat confusing and we would have to try to decipher which points could relate to our question. We need to be specific and ask questions such as 'What is the pain on the left side of my tummy?', 'What causes my indigestion when I am swallowing my food?' or 'What makes me depressed first thing in the morning?'. Each of these questions can receive a straightforward answer.

It is vital that the request is made mentally at least three times before sleeping. The theory is that the first request is just words, heard by the ego; the second is absorbed into the conscious awareness and the third repetition sinks into the deep unconscious. Also this repetition really helps to focus the mind. Some people like to write themselves a message on paper or draw a picture, which they then place under their pillow. It is also important to seed in dream remembrance simultaneously

(I will remember my dream when I wake in the morning). We can also request that sleep returns quickly if we are woken up before we have been given our answer.

For most people the greatest disappointment in dream incubation is the lack of immediate success. Do not be disillusioned. The mind is fickle. It has to be trained to operate at full capacity, like any other part of the body. We are so used to immediate simplistic answers to all our needs that we have become extremely impatient, giving up all too readily. Persist, persist, persist – like Robert the Bruce's spider.

Working with images

For some people thoughts or words are not enough to fully express how they are feeling. In these cases it is necessary to find an image. If you have a pain or a rash, a temperature or an upset digestion, spend some quiet time creating an image that you feel truly represents this malaise. An actual picture in your mind is not essential; imagining doesn't necessarily require pictures. Look for a congruent metaphor. A pain, for example, could be represented by the image of being stung by a bee, attacked by a scratching cat, or being hit with a hockey stick. It could be a pile driver, a burning flame, a prickly hedgehog. Alternatively it could be a large blob, a flowing red stream, a jangling of bright lights or even a loud discordant noise. What matters is that the image you choose really reflects the pain you feel. This image is then seeded into the dream state with a request to show you why the complaint is interfering with your life. The actual choice of image can also give you a good clue.

Let's look at an example of imagery in an incubated dream. Mary developed a rash on her hands similar to chilblains whenever they were exposed to persistent cold. This was a particular problem as her work involved handling frozen food. She imagined that her fingers resembled lumps of ice and incubated this into her dreams. She dreamed that she was sitting on the ice in the sunshine with some Eskimos, placing ice cubes into a saucepan and melting them over a fire into water. The dream clearly told her to warm her hands, which resembled blocks of ice. This, however, is what I call patching up. Constantly melting the ice cubes would not be a cure, merely a treatment or an alleviation, rather like a sticking plaster. The true cause was what was creating the ice cubes. In healing terms, this is known as the initial sensitizing event or ISE. It is the trigger that puts in motion the whole set of events. The problem here was not how to thaw out Mary's hands but how to prevent the freezing in the first place.

Mary subsequently asked how to prevent the freezing. Strangely she had almost the same dream but this time she was the Eskimo. Her hands were gloved and warm and she was melting ice for cooking some fish and milk. Here she was being given both the cause and the cure; she had not come to terms with her working environment and was being told to dress appropriately for her job. This was then able to put her in control in apparently totally harsh and alien conditions. Interestingly, fish and milk both contain calcium which is an old-fashioned remedy for chilblains.

Having established an image and worked with it leads to a deeper and more important stage. Mary used the melting of ice cubes as an image which her dreaming mind could work with. She established cause and effect. However, she also needed to look at the cause of the cause. To put it another way, an infected, suppurating boil might be caused, unknown to us, by a splinter. The first treatment would be to apply a poultice to clean out the pus and reduce the inflammation. However, although the treatment would ease the problem, without removing the splinter, the injury would not heal and would continue to fester.

Another instance of imagery occurred in an attempt to cure warts. John's chosen image was of a lot of balloons that had been inflated and deflated, leaving them limp and lumpy. He seeded these balloons into his dreams. He was rewarded with a dream where he was re-inflating them with hydrogen whereupon some of the balloons rose and floated away. In the morning, some of John's warts had disappeared as mysteriously as they had come. Repeated incubation eventually cured John's warts completely.

Working with words, affirmations and metaphors

Some people find it very difficult to come up with any images to crystallize their thoughts about the problem into anything but the obvious. They feel, as a consequence, that the dream method cannot be working for them. For such people affirmations could be the answer. So instead of, or even as a complement to, imagery, we can come up with a mental metaphor, an emotion, which we then ask the dream mind to develop for us. Common examples of affirmations are: 'I love myself. I am a useful and worthwhile person'; 'Every day my body becomes stronger and healthier'; 'Each morning the pain I am experiencing becomes less.' Another example of this would be when we have a cold in the head and can't breathe we can ask and seed 'What is getting up my nose?; or with backache 'Why don't I feel supported?' *You Can Heal Your Life* by Louise Hay contains many extremely good ideas along these lines.

Another aspect of the use of words has been discovered with the advent of neuro-linguistic programming. NLP has found that people respond to language differently, according to whether they are visual, auditory or kinaesthetic. If you use visual language to a visual person their understanding and response are immediate, whereas if you use auditory or kinaesthetic words misunderstanding can occur or the responses may be slower. The same applies to all three types. It is not a question of someone being stupid; it is just that the brain absorbs information differently. The way to recognize these different types is to listen carefully to how they express themselves. A visual person will say, 'I see you're looking better today.' An auditory person will say, 'I hear you're on good form today' while a kinaesthetic person will say, 'I can sense you're feeling better today.' Listen to how you express yourself and how you respond. Which type of person are you? Occasionally someone will be a mixture of more than one type but rarely all three. It is important that we use the right kind of sensory words for absorption when preparing our dream-seeding. We should use language that has a clear meaning to us. Chapters 8 and 9 give many examples of metaphors for illness to choose from. Read through these and find one that is appropriate to any current problem. Alternatively, they may well trigger metaphors of your own.

Working with colours and crystals

Some people find it helpful to introduce colours into their dream incubation. The attributes of the different colours are discussed in Chapter 12. For example if you are suffering from chronic tiredness adding red to your dream seed can have remarkable effects. Excessive stress can be treated with green and blue.

Placed under one's pillow, crystals are supposed to promote intuitive and inspired dreams. They help with sleeplessness and the pain of bereavement. Obsidian is supposed to be good for the eyes, cat's eye for skin diseases, topaz for blood pressure, moonstone for fluid control and garnet as an overall tonic. There are many more, details of which can be found in good books on the healing powers of crystals.

In our computer age we are familiar with the programming of quartz and silicon crystals. Quartz and rose quartz are the most frequently used healing crystals, since they can be 'programmed', that is, seeded with healing vibrations. They can protect naturally or through programming against viruses, infection and other ailments, making them invaluable in dream healing. They are accorded with powers of absorbency and protection, and can be programmed then placed to absorb negative atmospheres in homes, offices and public places. They can certainly be used to cleanse both the sleeping area and the whole of the home.

It is important to choose a crystal that appeals to you and to give it a good scrub with soap and water, leaving it to dry in the sunlight, before using it. Some people like to wash their crystals each time they ask a new question, to avoid possible confused responses. Before you go to sleep, hold the crystal in your hand and ask it to help you in your dreams. Keeping hold of the crystal, repeat your incubation idea three times, then place it under your pillow or beside your bed. Alternatively, you could make an arrangement of stones around the bed covering the four directions – top, bottom, left and right. This creates a special holding space which can be established by the mind as your dream healing environment.

Taking the technique further

Sometimes, despite everything, we still don't understand the meaning of an answer. In such a case we can incubate a repeat request into our next dreaming session asking for clarification. On other occasions the meaning might be quite clear, helping us and advising us what we need to do to cure ourselves. We can also take this a step further and incubate to check on the next course of action.

Re-incubation can be used when we do not understand the answer, when the answer is incomplete or when the situation is ongoing. In the first instance, maybe our request was not clear enough for a simple response. In this case we can either rephrase the question or request a clarification of the dream. In the second case, we can ask for the rest of the answer to our request or we can ask to re-enter the dream and allow it to reach its conclusion. On the last point, we may have asked initially for a simple diagnosis which the dream has provided and now we want to know the treatment. In this case we can incubate in instalments like a serial.

Sometimes we feel a dream is unfinished, and that we have not yet got the message. This can be handled in several ways. If we have the ability to fall directly back into sleep we can continue with the dream. Otherwise we can re-enter it later, asking our dream mind to return to the last dream and continue working on the previous seed, rather like a serial. In this instance it is also possible to decide whereabouts in the dream we wish to re-enter or even to ask for an action replay.

There is yet another technique that we can develop through dream seeding – that of dialoguing with the characters in our dreams, especially when using the re-entry technique. As you fall asleep, recall the dream and begin the conversation, letting it continue as you drop off. What is important here is what is known as immersion – complete and total concentration on the seed.

The Lucid Dreaming Technique

Lucid dreaming is the ability to be asleep and dreaming while being totally aware that you are asleep and dreaming. We can acquire this skill through dream incubation, but do understand that it takes time. You need to ask the dream mind to let you know when it is dreaming, so that you can become the outside observer and director of what is going on.

Although altering dreams, especially nightmares, can bring about real relief, bear in mind that when you dream your unconscious mind is trying to tell you something. So if you train yourself to practise lucid dreaming and start altering too many of your dreams, you could miss important messages and merely develop a fantasy world or playground for your own imagination. It is important, therefore, to realize what the initial message of the dream is and deal with that first.

On the other hand, being a spontaneous lucid dreamer must, in itself, have a message. The whole purpose of spontaneous lucid dreaming is to make the appropriate alterations and possibly to reprogramme the unconscious mind. It gives an opportunity to try out new ways of being or to experiment with different outcomes to fit one's current lifestyle. It is yet another unknown ability of the brain that we are only just exploring.

Lucid dreams are often preceded by sensations of flying or floating and a clear knowledge that one is dreaming. Dr Keith Hearne, the British dream scientist, has done considerable research on training people to dream lucidly and he identifies a number of clear clues:

- dreaming of being unable to turn on a light, or any kind of electrical equipment malfunctioning
- finding you are flying
- having the ability to penetrate solid objects
- finding you are able to move things around at will and change the action of the dream.

If lucid dreaming is not a natural experience for us, we can use incubation to achieve this state nightly by requesting the dream mind to allow us to be the director of our dreams, to truly know what it is like to be inside the dream. It takes a lot of practice to dream lucidly, so don't be fooled by those who say you can achieve it in days. In dream laboratories volunteers are constantly woken from the REM state to try to make them aware of being in a dream.

Once we have achieved this skill, we can use incubation or dream seeding in conjunction with lucidity. Here we can direct the solution to a given problem so that the outcome is truly comfortable. For example, to deal with a phobia about spiders, we could use a lucid dream either to make ourselves grow in size so that the spider disappears into insignificance or we could reduce the spider until barely visible. In either case fears can be eliminated. For healing, in the lucid state we can discover the best medicine for our needs. We could see ourselves in the doctor's surgery and watch him writing a prescription for our cure, or go to a pharmacy and ask which medicine we need.

Dr Hearne discovered that physical stressors are apparent in the sleep state. There is tension and apprehension, particularly with people suffering from such diseases as asthma. Just prior to an attack bodily changes take place; the breathing becomes restricted which leads to a sense of panic. Using dream incubation, the unconscious mind can be alerted early to these signs, waking the sleeper before the crisis is reached. Diagnostic dreams can also be seeded to be triggered by the physical changes before the panic stage. Many asthmatics have benefited from this self-healing treatment.

6

••••••••••••••••••••••

Dream Healing (2) – Recording and Interpretation

Keeping a Dream Journal

'How can I remember my dreams?' is a common cry. If you feel that you never dream or have trouble remembering your dreams, follow the incubation procedure. Every night as you are waiting to fall asleep, concentrate on your desire to remember your dreams. Programme your unconscious mind to remember. Tell it that it will remember in the morning.

Try writing your wish to remember on a piece of paper and place it under your pillow. This is exactly the same method suggested for incubating dreams to answer problems. Then the moment you wake, write down whatever is in your mind. It doesn't matter how silly it appears to be. Responses may be slow at first, but don't despair. Even the most reluctant minds produce information in the end. Just keep repeating your request each night.

Buy yourself a dream journal. This can be a simple notebook, a tape recorder or dictaphone (if you sleep alone) or a loose-leaf folder containing pages with the headings shown on page 67. Decorate and personalize your dream journal to make it special. You will also need a torch and something to write with. The moment you wake, write down anything you can remember – words, colours, impressions. The waking mind releases the night images almost immediately, so any delay can be your undoing. Write down the important features first, because the whole dream will take time to record. It is easy to become so absorbed in the details of the beginning that you forget that all-important answer to the question. A few crucial and pertinent words will help to hold the entire sequence so that you can elaborate at your leisure.

There are several reasons for keeping a dream journal. Firstly, it helps us understand what the dream mind is trying to say and thus put it to use, and secondly, it allows us to look for any patterns that emerge over a period of time. We may discover that memorable dreams only occur around the full moon, on the 15th of each month, when meeting a certain person or before a difficult interview. The pattern may not necessarily be logical or easily identified – each one of us responds to a personal time cycle. However, identifying a pattern is particularly useful when incubating a dream for an important answer. The request can be timed to coincide with the most fertile dreaming period.

Keeping a dream journal may reveal the same dream or one expressing a similar set of circumstances happening whenever certain situations occur in waking life. Recognizing the pattern helps us deal better with whatever the recurring problem may be. Forewarned is forearmed. All of our emotions and fears are hidden in our dream language.

Annwn discovered that she had her most powerful dreams around the full moon. She was suffering from deep depression following a break-up with her partner of six years. She timed concentration on her dreams to coincide with the full moon:

I was told to look in a mirror. To do this I had to walk naked through a room full of people including my ex-partner and his new girlfriend. I felt sad and his girlfriend looked sad. She kept repeating, 'I do look good, don't I?' I arrived in a room full of mirrors containing reflections of a happy radiant person. I studied them and suddenly realized they were me and was filled instantaneously with great self-confidence. This wonderful feeling has stayed with me. I feel positive and peaceful.

A dream journal needs to show the date and the major occurrences of the previous and subsequent days. These will indicate if the dream is the answer to a current problem. It may be just a review, or it may be telling us how to deal with what has or what will happen, rather than giving an overview of the next period in our life. We are looking for patterns and also for responses.

Adding waking details shows just how much we are influenced or victimized by our outside circumstances. It also reveals when we are feeling below par. Some people get early warnings of such illnesses as colds, flu or headaches. In the same way, I know an elderly lady who examines her lifestyle when she gets an illness. She discovers what is bothering her and deals with it, and then the illness goes away. This has worked with shingles and fibroids. 'I don't really need them,' she says. Thus the simple keeping of a dream journal can have a number of healing benefits, by revealing emotional connections with illness.

Keep a separate section for repetitions – recurring dreams and recurring symbols, images or situations. It only needs to be one page but it will throw up patterns much more clearly.

Dream Interpretation

The first thing to write down is an outline of the dream while it is still fresh in your mind. Keep it really brief, because forgetting is almost automatic. Very occasionally, a dream may remain with you all day or even longer. This happens when the message needs hammering home and the dream mind feels that the conscious mind is refusing to acknowledge what it is being shown. Alternatively, this can indicate a precognitive dream.

Having got the bare bones on paper, elaborate on it as much as necessary. The headings listed below should be completed where relevant if the meaning of the dream is not immediately clear.

Here is a very simple dream related to our journey through life, a common theme in dreams. 'I am walking tall through the forest without hesitation. I can see where I am going along a straight pathway.' Let us now take the building blocks of this scenario:

Direction straight forward   *Method* walking   *Effort* easy
Attitude confident   *Direction of vision* forward

We can interpret this as saying that our current path through life is direct. We have clear goals and we feel confident.

Here is another dream sequence using exactly the same scenario, but to this dreamer the imagery has an entirely different meaning. 'I am creeping through a forest. The path winds and I cannot see clearly ahead. I have to bend my head to avoid low branches. I am afraid and want to turn back. There is a noise and I hide behind a large oak.' Applying the above criteria we have the following:

Direction winding	*Method* creeping	*Effort* hesitant
Attitude nervous	*Direction of vision* ahead but obstructed	

Here the journey through life is entirely different. It shows the dreamer is of a nervous disposition, without clear goals (because the path winds), prefers to hide rather than confront difficulties and is fearful of putting much effort into achieving anything. Thus by analysing how we are making a dream journey we can associate it with our current lifestyle and begin to see how it fits.

These are simple examples of dream analysis. More detailed interpretations can be made by making up pages in your journal in advance, using the same headings for each page, and filling them in each morning. Below are two examples of how this might work. The first example (*opposite*) is a recurring dream about buildings.

A possible interpretation of Example 1 would be that the dreamer is feeling hunger (either for food, love or attention of some sort) and the kitchen is a source of nourishment (or starvation). The front door is an access from a safe environment to the outside world, while dogs usually represent friends. This suggests that the dreamer is feeling neglected and has retreated inside herself but has left the door open for friends. They come but merely make use of what the dreamer has to offer rather than giving real friendship, leaving her still in need.

Example 1

Today's date: Sat 12th

Main event yesterday: *Lunch with friends.* **Next main event:** *Giving a party.*

BRIEF RÉSUMÉ OF DREAM

I feel hungry so I go to the kitchen. Then the front door bursts open and I am invaded by dogs who, ignoring me, eat up all my food. There is nothing left for me.

INCUBATED: No **SEED:** *None.*

TYPE: Healing, Incubated, Wish-fulfilment, Serial/Creative, Nightmare, <u>Recurring</u>, Lucid, Precognitive, Sexual, Other _____

TIME: Past, <u>Present</u>, Future, Day, Night, Dawn, Midday, Evening, Midnight, Spring, Summer, Autumn, Winter, Childhood, Historical, Far Memory, Other _____

JOURNEY: *None.*

ATMOSPHERE/OWN FEELINGS: *Feeling hungry, being ignored, left with nothing.*

BUILDINGS: *In the kitchen, hall and front door.*

PEOPLE/ANIMALS: *Dogs.*

OBJECTS/COLOURS: *Food, empty plates.*

WORDS/PUNS: *None.*

The second example (*opposite*) shows how the same framework can be used to interpret an incubated dream.

The dreamer here has no control and is virtually turning into yellowy brown liquid, being melted down. The maniac is what the dreamer is ingesting, which is creating the fluid. Because this is an incubated dream, it would seem that there could be an outbreak of diarrhoea from bad food in their work canteen. The dreamer will not be the only one to suffer.

Problems with interpretation

The most important thing to realize when trying to interpret dreams is that generally the sequence of the storyline is only partially to do with the meaning. This is why they frequently seem so bizarre. Virtually every image in a dream means something else. For example, a father is not a father – he is about authority or kindness or protection. Which aspect he represents depends upon our feelings for our own father or a father substitute. Each one of us has a personal interpretation of everything according to our own experiences, which works in pictures or images – call it personal hieroglyphics. The message is in the image representation. Thus if we take the various images and replace them with their hidden meanings, the correct storyline appears. We have to search our memory banks to understand our own symbols.

Dreams can be difficult to understand due to the symbology of the dream itself, but they may also be complete gobbledegook, in which case we need to incubate a request for a translation in our next dream session. The other important factor to look out for is puns. Dreams often contain metaphors from our everyday language: feeling blue, being crabby, dog-in-a-manger, and so on. These particular metaphors could manifest in dreams by blue being a dominant colour, or by a crab or a dog being a main character. Obvious features like these should be taken both literally and metaphorically.

Example 2

Today's date: Mon 12

Main event yesterday: *Discussion at work about the canteen.*   **Next main event:**

BRIEF RÉSUMÉ OF DREAM

I'm on a conveyor belt controlled by a gloating maniac, moving towards a deep vat. We turn into liquid and I feel myself hitting thick yellow brown liquid. I think that's it. I'm gone. I saw the maniac stirring the liquid around with a stick.

INCUBATED: Yes   **SEED:** *Worrying about stomach problems.*

TYPE: Healing, <u>Incubated</u>, Wish-fulfilment, Serial/Creative, Nightmare, Recurring, Lucid, Precognitive, Sexual, Other _____

TIME: Past, <u>Present</u>, Future, Day, Night, Dawn, Midday, Evening, Midnight, Spring, Summer, Autumn, Winter, Childhood, Historical, Far Memory, Other _____

JOURNEY: *On conveyor belt. Journeying with others.*

ATMOSPHERE/OWN FEELINGS: *Feeling afraid and weak and turning to water, being out of control with the situation.*

BUILDINGS: *None.*

PEOPLE/ANIMALS: *With others, maniac in control.*

OBJECTS/COLOURS: *Conveyor belt, large vat, yellowy brown.*

WORDS/PUNS: *None.*

Because the dream mind only works in imagery it often helps with interpretation to treat the dream like a comic strip, especially if it appears to be absolute nonsense. Reduce the main features into pictures and write underneath each its individual meaning:

Kitchen – need nourishment.	Hall – transition to outside. Dogs – friends. Ignore me.	Eat food. Don't share. Ignore me.	Leave. Empty plates. Ignore me.
I'm hungry and go looking for food.	I keep hoping that my so-called friends will visit. When they do I feel invisible.	So-called friends use me, finding satisfaction at my expense, giving nothing in return.	My life is very empty and very lonely.

We mentioned earlier the apparent non-dream. This is when we have nothing in the morning to indicate that our seeding has been acknowledged. When this happens we need to be on the lookout for synchronicities during the following days. For example, the day after an incubated dream you might become very aware of kettles wherever you go – in your kitchen, at the office, in shop windows. In fact, they seem to be everywhere you turn. You may ask why such a thing as a kettle could have any importance. Think how often we use boiling water as a metaphor in our waking life. It conjures up an immediate image to clarify a situation. So notice whether the kettles are at boiling point – about to explode like an angry outburst. Or are they off the boil – in other words lukewarm and no longer reaching maximum power, showing lassitude or lack of energy? Are they slow coming to the boil – a sign of weakness or depression? Or are they not functioning at all, simply passive?

All these examples can relate directly to an illness or run-down body. We need to clarify what the kettles are doing most often to find the diagnostic pointer.

One surprisingly common example of the message coming the following day is when a song repeatedly comes to mind and will not go away. Instead of dismissing it as an irritation, listen to the words. What are they saying to you?

When you are struggling without much success to understand your dream language, try free association. This method was used by Freud and Jung, and involves taking the main image or word and then writing down the first word that comes into your head. Having done that, write the next one that springs spontaneously to mind. Continue to do this until something clicks and the underlying meaning of the dream becomes apparent. Again this association can be seeded.

If a dream keeps repeating itself it means that we simply are not getting the message. We need to be more alert when we are awake. It could also be that we do not want to listen or can't be bothered to make the necessary changes. We could perhaps call them nagging dreams – our conscience getting at us.

Of course there are times when we have straightforward literal dreams. These dreams are those that seem to be a review or a continuation of whatever has happened to us during the day. The main point that distinguishes them is the lack of symbolism. Often we can refuse to accept a dream at face value and spend many hours trying to read something into it which isn't there. For example, I dreamed I was going out and could not find my car keys. After a prolonged search, I found them on the hook where they should have been. It would be easy to try to read special meanings into this dream, but the truth of the matter is that this is exactly what happens to me on many occasions.

7

•••••••••••••••••••••

Understanding
Dream Imagery

Dreaming consists of a series of images or impressions which present themselves when the mind is relaxed and in an altered state of consciousness, when it is not operating in a highly active state and when the brainwaves are slowing down. These images are part of ourselves and surface from the unconscious mind as a result, in the main, of experiences registered in our memories, and also from a form of ancestral memory which we all share.

We draw on images in response to our needs or circumstances. For example, when listening to the radio or reading fiction we create for ourselves an entire world in images and are frequently disappointed when actors' faces are put to radio voices or we see a dramatization of a book in which the producer's concept does not match our own. But where does our imagery come from? How is it formed?

The Early Learning Period

Think of the mind of a new-born child as an area of well-prepared fertile ground, unsullied by any growth. As the child draws its first breath it begins to experience. Each new experience is like a seed being planted. There is no discrimination between good seeds or weeds. Whenever a seed is dropped it can put down roots.

However, when an experience is repeated or has a resemblance to a previous one, a new facet of the mind comes into play. Recognition occurs and the first yardsticks of discrimination are created. If the repeat experience contradicts an existing example in some way it is rejected. If the recognition is acceptable it is like sprinkling fertilizer on the soil and the plant grows stronger. Through the repetition a memory has been compounded. The mind can now discriminate, being aware that differences exist. For example, when a child is presented with a loaf and told it is called *bread*, he does not question this. Had you used another word, say *tomato*, the child would have accepted it, having no reason to think otherwise. Doubt would only enter the equation if he was confronted by other people adamantly telling him that he was misinformed. Even then, it would take time to accept the error.

Sowing seeds in virgin soil, however, is simplicity itself. It is the entrenchment time, when deep truths and misconceptions can be sown. This process continues with each and every brand new experience throughout life.

Memory and the Unconscious Mind

The first manifestation of memory is the measuring stick. If we haven't experienced something, we have no personal means of assessment. We have to burn our fingers to understand the concept of being burnt and a parent's warnings, although possibly delaying the experience, have no true reality. Thus the memory exists as a filter between the conscious and the unconscious, and is based on recognition. Thus any information fed in during the early non-discriminatory stages becomes very well established.

So we can see that early learning is much more important than is generally realized, since it is from this stage in our lives that most associations are created. And yet these early years can be a most neglected time of a child's education. We tend to underestimate – and perhaps do not even understand – the profundity of the child's absorption capabilities. It is during these early years that the most damage is done. First impressions cannot be eradicated, only modified. A child's mind is like a sponge; its absorption is indiscriminate. We carry with us throughout our life what we absorb during this early learning period – and some of it is like excess luggage, a constant impediment.

So what is it that we are storing away? What are memories? They appear to be records of things and how we relate to them. A memory of a chair is about its shape, its colour, its construction, its purpose – but there is also generally an emotion. If, for example, we recall a lounge chair from our childhood home, with the recollection also come the memories of who sat in it, together with memories of good and bad times. The image comes into the conscious mind, bringing with it all its associations.

It appears that all conscious experiences go to the unconscious and surface, bidden or unbidden, triggered by the memory. Thus it could be said that all consciousness is the memory in operation. Everything new is bounced off it.

Memory seems to act as a picture library for dreams. Its language is images, such as the above-mentioned chair. Frequently, however, the message it is trying to put across is not about the chair but about the abstracts connected with it. Imagine that the chair in our example was our mother's favourite, where she sat relaxing after a long, hard day. For the dream mind the chair does not literally mean a chair. It is telling us that the motherly, caring part of ourselves needs to sit back and relax.

So this is how our dream library is created. We develop a personal language composed of a series of individual hieroglyphics or, in modern idiom, computer graphics. These pictures are assembled as we dream to express our emotional state. This is why dreams frequently seem so bizarre. There does not have to be an obvious progressive flow. What appears to be a random selection of pictures has a hidden sequence in the underlying emotions or circumstances connected with each image.

Another factor is that the unconscious mind appears out of reach of our waking selves. It holds instinctual memory and controls our automatic responses. It will react without deliberate intervention and thus can dominate our actions and emotions, causing a feeling of helplessness and lack of control in our waking lives, all of which is strengthened through compounding. It operates on a deeper level and it is through dreams that we can make contact with it.

The unconscious mind is a databank of fixed ideas and actions outside the realm of reason. Once a fact has registered and become a memory, removing it is very difficult – some might say impossible. New patterns cannot be learnt where the memory only acknowledges worn-out patterns and values. It is important to understand that nothing can be erased, only modified. This leads to the need for a modification process to deal with this storehouse of true and false impressions. This in turn brings us back to dream incubation. Through this technique we can access the pattern in the memory and offer alternatives, and when a change feels comfortable this slightly altered image will become part of, and enrich, the original image.

The Collective Unconscious

The collective unconscious is the name given by Jung to an area of the mind that we seem to be able to access in dreaming and daydreaming. To give an example, scientific discoveries take place simultaneously in different laboratories worldwide where the research has been kept absolutely secret. How does it come about that separate groups are chasing the same discoveries? All we know is that when we are thinking deeply, mulling over problems, dropping into the daydream/dream mode, we seem to be able to tap into this weird and undefinable space.

Another example of this is found in writing and journalism, where the frequent cry is 'they stole my idea'. Personally, I have found that if I have a new idea, it is important for me to develop it quickly and *not* speak about it. It is as though discussing it sends it out on the ether and allows others to develop it before me. It's as though somewhere there is a giant listening aerial, picking up thoughts. However, it is more likely that this idea is already 'out there' and I am just one of the receivers tuning in, meaning I have to act quickly.

We also seem to have a form of racial memory which could come from DNA. DNA contains an unbroken link to the depths of our ancestry. So it is likely to manifest in some instinctual manner, like bringing out family characteristics in members who have lived apart all their lives, rather like a behavioural telepathic link. It should be observed, however, that DNA can only carry its own experience and this is generally limited by the age of the parents at the time of conception.

The collective unconscious also comprises certain instinctual levels of being that are common to all humanity in that they invoke similar responses in everyone. Jung named these 'archetypal energies', many of which humankind anthropomorphized into gods and goddesses. Any examination of mythology shows that these beings represent, and are names for, attitudes and behaviours. The many pantheons that exist worldwide show parallels. Each tradition has its father, mother and son, its shadow, its scryer, its oracle, its mystic, its priest, its healer, and so on. Each represents an aspect of archetypal energy. So once again images are used to represent abstracts – emotions and responses.

The Archetypes and the Human Psyche

According to Jung our personalities have certain distinct characteristics. Whether male or female, we have both a feminine side (the anima) and a masculine side (the animus). Since we clearly manifest our gender in our waking lives, it is left to the dream world to bring in guidance and the balancing effect. For example, a weak ineffectual woman who is obliged to take some positive action will often dream of a strong, efficient man, indicating the need to develop that side of herself. Sometimes the dream may be more subtle, and the man may appear incompetent, but then through skill and mental agility overcome his adversaries. Here the woman is being shown that she needs to call on and combine her masculine side with her stronger feminine resources to find her answers. The same applies for men who may dream of women when they need to soften their approach and use more feminine wiles to get their own way.

Thus the animus is the masculine, dominant and practical side of the female developed from her contact with the males in her family. She takes this image, this 'man of her dreams' and tries to superimpose it on all men that she meets. The same applies to the anima for the man, developed from his relationship with his mother and other females. How frequently do we come across the husband projecting his mother image onto the wife and vice versa?

The ego tends to appear to dominate, but frequently is only an observer, rather like us looking at ourselves. The shadow represents those parts of ourselves that we refuse to confront. In *A Dictionary for Dreamers*, Tom Chetwynd suggests that we bring to mind the person we detest most in the world, and blend with them the nastiest side of anyone else we know, in order to get a realistic impression of our own shadow. The shadow is reflected in the people whom we most dislike or envy in our waking lives. This dark side epitomizes our projections. I learned quite early on that the things I dislike most in other people are actually my own worst faults. But this is not necessarily ugly; it simply represents the other side of the coin.

So the first thing we need to discover is what aspect of ourselves this person or persons represent. This is often difficult to identify so it is worth looking at the archetypal energies that they may represent. We are many-faceted and virtually all the characteristics mentioned below manifest within us at some time or another. See if you can recognize yourself.

The feminine principle

To many people, the feminine is the epitome of the Goddess principle. What generally springs first into our minds is the wise old woman, the mother earth, our feminine connection with the source of all wisdom and the collective unconscious. She is the one we turn to in our greatest need, especially as the mediator between us and the supreme creative forces.

The feminine principle manifests in terms of certain qualities. It is seen as wise, nurturing, ingenuous, receptive, intuitive, deep-thinking, sensitive, emotional, gentle, feeling, caring, mysterious, virginal, flirtatious. We also see the obverse, the terrible mother who disciplines us, the earth that erupts around us – rigid, domineering, possessive, narrow-minded, naïve, weak, cold, hard, uncaring, sensual, erotic, bewitching, scheming, evil.

The feminine principle manifests in four main guises, each of which has two faces. The roles it plays are as follows.

The Mother (the Matron) – expansion/absorption

We are all familiar with the Mother image – the Virgin Mary, a mother rocking her child to sleep, 'rubbing it better', suckling a baby, preparing food in the kitchen, taking the children to school, doing chores such as shopping or cleaning. All these images are about nurturing, caring and being gently protective.

The Mother has another face. She can be excessively aggressive, especially in defence. She can be possessive, or pathetically demanding. She can be completely neglectful, self-absorbed and uncaring. She can refuse to break the ties and allow her chicks to fly. She devours.

So when we dream of a Mother figure, first of all we need to ask ourselves what she means to us. Which of these categories does she fit into? What was our relationship with our own mother, or to the mothers of our friends? Do we need to be more caring or are we devouring, suffocating those around us?

Female bosses and mothers-in-law can come in this category.

The Maiden (the Princess) – youth, spontaneity/eroticism

This is the princess of all our fairytales. She is the image of unsullied youthfulness. She expresses lightness and happiness. She is the young heroine full of bright expectations who has not yet experienced the realities of adult life. She is still in the virginal state, but can also be the naïve unmarried mother.

Her other side is the streetwise youngster, the girl who is old before her time. Maybe she has had to mother her brothers and sisters. There is often a wildness about her. She is found in the role of the seductress (Lolita), the prostitute or the deliberate unmarried mother.

When this character appears in your dreamscape, look at that part of yourself, whatever your age. The maiden can appear in later life when we need to re-experience these parts of ourselves. Are we yearning for that young, naïve time when we were free from responsibilities – or were able to get away with or refusing to accept them. Perhaps we are making our lives too complicated and need to get back to basics. We may need to cultivate these maiden-like qualities. On the other hand, perhaps we are being too naïve and should be drawing more on our maturity. For mothers, this image can represent some aspect of their relationships with their daughters. Frequently, there is an unrecognized role-reversal. Alternatively the image may be connected with workmates, friends or simply fantasies or desires.

Sisters, nieces, daughters-in-law, girlfriends and female colleagues fall in this category.

The Mature Woman – positive/negative intellect
In her positive form, she is the blue-stocking, the deep intellectual; she is frequently a spinster and is often inward-looking. She is the maiden aunt, the governess, the career woman dedicated to her work. She also appears as the mother whose children have grown and left, who is totally absorbed with herself, or who does good works to fill the gaps in her life. In the main there is an imbalance in this personality. The predominant features are a need to manage without men or to treat them as inferior beings.

Her other form is that of the huntress. She uses her intellect to entrap and, although dismissive of men, uses all forms of seduction to gain her ends. She makes all the overtures. She is a dominant and powerful personality who thinks nothing of trampling people under foot and tossing them away when they have outlived their usefulness. She can also be seen in the woman who deliberately sets out to have affairs, with a sort of frenetic intensity. She can be described as 'mutton dressed as lamb' – the older woman pretending to be a teenager, unable to accept the ageing process. Usually, despite her reputation, men cannot resist her because in many ways she represents their latent need for a mother and the off-loading of responsibility – the woman in charge. She allows them to take without concerning themselves with the consequences.

When this aspect appears in your dreams, ask yourself if you are becoming too immersed in your work. Are you sharing enough? Have you become so absorbed that you are losing a clear perspective, leading to imbalance? Are there big gaps in your life? Alternatively, are you chasing males simply for a one-night stand and consequently avoiding any long-term commitments? Perhaps you feel over-stressed and foetal and simply want to close your eyes and leave all the problem-solving to others.

Aunts, older sisters, friends, mothers-in-law, female bosses and workmates come in this category.

The Priestess/the Sorceress – intuitive good/intuitive evil
These females can appear in any relationship to you. This is the intuitive side of the feminine. These people seem capable of taking an overall objective view of a situation. They are very clear-thinking and are not open to coercion or narrow-minded manipulation. They always seem to have the answers but you cannot depend on them because they tend to disappear when you least expect it. There is a distinct feeling that they have contact with powers elsewhere since they invariably make all the right decisions. Frequently they either will not or cannot rationalize.

The obverse here is the schemer, the woman who ever so

casually destroys with a word, who drips poison in her gossip, damns with faint praise. She is the character annihilator who finds fault wherever she goes – always, of course, for the 'best of reasons' and in the 'nicest possible way'. Surprisingly, she is often a 'do-gooder' since this role can be taken on for self-aggrandisement rather than altruism.

When these ladies appear in your dreams, try to see your motives really clearly. It is important to distinguish between objective action for general good and manipulative action for self-benefit.

The masculine principle

It is important to realize that the masculine is not the opposite of the feminine, but the complement. As with the female, each aspect of the male has its obverse side. The wise old man is the epitome of all the positive principles of the animus. He is God the father, the source of all cosmic wisdom, the overall creator, the mentor. He is the character on whom we call and to whom we pray when in need, the external father principle, the ultimate adviser and protector. In his negative guise, he is the wrathful God, exacting penalties for misbehaviour. He is without mercy.

The Father – protection/fear

In the main, the Father represents the provider. He is the hunter/gatherer who preserves the race and procreates. His main roles in the family environment are those of authority, provision and protection. He also represents ideals and standards to live up to. We look up to him with respect and seek his approval.

His other face is to be feared. This is the authoritarian character, the one who brooks no argument. He has no time for you or your opinions. He is frequently sadistic and uncaring, taking punishment and cruelty to extremes. He is the oppressive ogre who deprives us of individuality. He can also be the sex abuser.

So when the Father appears in your dreams, recall which of

the above describes your father. What is he actually representing for you? Either there is a trait in yourself that needs attention or else there is an external force infiltrating into your everyday life. Is the authority benign or threatening?

Fathers, uncles, older brothers, fathers-in-law, bosses and dominating friends are in this category.

The Hero (Prince)/the Wastrel (Lout) – action/inaction

The Hero is the young man with high ideals, setting out on the quest of life. He is young, strong, idealistic and naïve, fresh and untarnished. He is also the dreamer or poet, capable of great achievements. He has great personal belief in himself, his ideas and his intention to change the world. As a lover, he is more platonic than passionate and offers chaste kisses.

His other aspect is the Wastrel, the vagabond, the one who thinks the world owes him a living. Or he can appear as the Lout, constantly disrupting the order of things. He has no desire to make any contribution and frequently, like Peter Pan, remains in a state of eternal childhood and irresponsibility. He tends to indulge in prolonged procrastination and untidiness. Sex for him is a form of physical gratification.

Brothers, boyfriends, nephews, sons-in-law, workmates and weak bosses come into this category.

The Warrior/the Villain – positive/negative intellect

The Warrior is the mature man of experience who has suffered the knocks and bruises of life. He is worldly-wise but on a mundane rather than a spiritual level. He shows considerable vitality and aggressiveness, being prepared to take on all comers. He can be very protective and possessive, absorbed with materialism and personal gain. He is frequently the teacher.

The Villain has several guises. He may appear as the uncouth rogue who lives by his wits or as a blunderer blindly trampling over everything in front of him. Another face, however, is the sophisticated cheat or trickster who also makes negative use of his intellect. He often makes use of his maturity to dupe those younger and more innocent than himself.

Colleagues, uncles, brothers, nephews and sons-in-law are found in this category.

The High Priest/the Black Magician – intuitive good/intuitive evil

This archetype can occur in any relationship to you. The High Priest represents very high ideals and seems to obtain his wisdom from higher sources. He knows without any need for logical reasoning. He is the way-shower through the tangled paths of life. He has a tendency to be ritualistic, yet is quite objective and altruistic. He can be seen as the mentor, guru or personal guide.

Alternatively the Black Magician is the megalomaniac. Everything he does is purely for personal gain. He uses every means he can to achieve his own ends. He deliberately mesmerizes and uses others' innocence for his own benefit, regardless of the cost. He looks for followers to brainwash and form his power base. He is very subtle and is seldom recognized for what he is, having almost vampire-like tendencies.

The Fool/the Jester/the Clown

This is an interesting personality since it is generally a disguise. If we consider Shakespeare's conception of the Fool, we see that really he is the wise man ('many a true word spoken in jest'). He uses laughter and joking to lighten heavy situations and atmospheres. In his 'apparent' naïveté he can 'rush in where angels fear to tread', virtually forcing others to look at situations from a different angle. It is never wise to dismiss the Fool without examination.

However, he does have another face – that of the genuine Fool, constantly making a fool of himself. You will observe him in the eternal joker whose strenuous and artificial humour is tedious in the extreme. He is not funny or even clever. This type of behaviour is a cry for help, a desperate need for attention at any cost.

The Child

The Child in the main epitomizes innocence, inquisitiveness, absorption and growth. It is like an unwritten book or something malleable which can be shaped to the will and ideals of others. The Child is like a sponge, absorbing and being affected by whatever it comes in contact with. Out of this myriad of experiences it grows. Its very innocence has a wisdom about it which frequently seems to be well beyond its years.

The other face of the Child is that of disruption and hyper-activity. On this level, innocence is replaced by a wily cunning. In fact, some children are distinctly evil. They are even quite sexually aware. They will deliberately stimulate without a clear understanding of the likely outcome.

Much work can be done on the Inner Child who has frequently been abused, whether mentally, physically, environ-mentally or morally – in fact, on all levels of its being. Very few of us have come through childhood unscathed by some form of negative indoctrination.

Mythical Beasts

The human imagination has invented mythical creatures as a way of explaining the unexplainable. They are also thought to have archetypal significance. A number of cultures combine animals with humans to create a blend of different characteristics.

We invent monsters as a way of dealing with our fears. They can take any shape or form but are often related to our early experiences with myth and fairytale, and nowadays television and film. They clearly indicate a refusal to face up to our terrors in waking life.

The centaur is a combination of man and horse. It comprises the intelligence and skills of the man superimposed on the speed and drive of the horse, and represents the lower instinctual side manipulated by the intellectual. The Pegasus, or flying horse, is a messenger and reflects the lower energies attempting to lighten and transform themselves.

The dragon occurs in cultures throughout the world and is thought to be a flying version of the serpent. Some see it as epitomizing good and others evil. It can represent the life force and sexual energies, while at the same time having the purifying and transforming qualities of fire. It can also represent deep inner fears, and the slaying of a dragon is an extremely powerful image. Dragons frequently guard treasure, so dealing with them in the dream world can bring about great release and discovery of things you did not know you possessed.

The phoenix rises up out of the ashes, and so is about transformation and rebirth. Sometimes we need to symbolically destroy all of our present circumstances and metamorphose from the remains into something fresh and new.

The unicorn is one of the most famous of the mythical beasts and usually represents purity, virginity and altruism, although for some people it is phallic and symbolizes sexuality. It can be both aggressive and gentle. Its horn was at one time thought to have water-divining properties, and it was reputed to have the ability to detect and extract poison. It is a lunar image and appears in heraldry as the polar opposite of the lion.

Other Beings

Since time immemorial angels have appeared in dreams as messengers. Instances of this are well-recorded in the Bible. Sometimes they can be interpreted as a guardian angel or even one's higher self. Their usual meaning is that of being uplifted and connecting with higher levels of consciousness.

Most of the well-known angels are archangels and some are recognizable as such. If they appear in your dreams, listen to what they have to say, as well as looking for the underlying messages of any associations.

Aliens frequently appear in dreams nowadays and usually indicate that the dreamer is straying into unfamiliar territory, where things are strange and unrecognizable. They can also be guides bringing messages from apparently external levels of consciousness. Generally we need to learn their language and tread carefully, rather than be dismissive.

Royalty and celebrities are common in dreams and usually indicate a need for fame or recognition. Being in the presence of such people also emphasizes one's own insignificance. However, do not forget that theatrical people are not what they seem. They are playing a part and can be presenting a false image.

Ancestors usually indicate a need to look into our past for answers. We are all the culmination of the lifetimes of many generations, and through our genes we have access to all the experiences of those before us. It is quite a remarkable thought. This enables us to have far memory dreams and to explore past life regressions. Thus when we dream of ancestors or grandparents, we are being asked to look backwards and draw on the past to help with today's problems.

Ghosts are apparitions which haunt us; this is the clue to their significance in dreams. They represent something that we are unable to let go of. Thus they hang around, appearing each time a pattern is repeated. They are also things which we can see right through, and can represent seeing through illusions. Understanding their source helps to release them. Excessive grieving can lead to holding onto the spirits of those who have died, forging strong chains of guilt and worry for the migrating soul. Dreams help us to recognize this and sever the links.

Very occasionally, ghosts may be sent to us through an outside thought from one who is thinking constantly about us. These hauntings are not necessarily negative or evil, just uncomfortable. The simple way to deal with them is to ask quietly and firmly that they return whence they came.

8

•••••••••••••••••••••••

Understanding Our Dreams (1) – Body Systems

This chapter explores the major dream symbols, the subconscious topics around which we weave all our emotions, hopes and fears. Remembering that all our images are our own inventions drawn from our personal experiences, if we take these themes as clues, we can then use common sense to find out how the images interweave.

Body Puns and Metaphors

The body is probably the most used dream symbol, each part of it representing some emotional trauma. In a way every physical ailment is a metaphor for an unconscious thought pattern, a manifestation of an attitude which begins in the mind. The simple way to understand this is to take each body part in turn and look at its several meanings, to which we can add our own personal ones. See how body parts are represented in your dreams and interpret this association. Look for puns. Thus, when we dream we have a cold in the nose we can ask, 'What is getting up my nose?'. This simple question could bring an immediate realization of some disorder in one's lifestyle. Catching a cold is rather like being shouted at by someone because you are refusing to listen. It's a warning signal that should put us on alert and often appears in dreams long before a real illness develops. Usually, however, we are too blinkered to notice. Very many illnesses respond to understanding these metaphors. So it is important to search for one which feels right and, if there is no immediate realization of the underlying circumstances, seed this idea into the dream state for analysis.

An example of this type of pun would be a dream about 'split hairs' which might show that we are too pedantic. At the same time we could have actual split ends in our hair which could be giving the same message. It is remarkable how often the facts and the analogy are interrelated. In this case, being less critical in our waking lives, while at the same time adopting a caring attitude towards our hair, should lead to the problem resolving itself.

Problems can also come to our attention the other way round. We might, for example, have split ends which do not respond to standard treatment. We might then ask our dream mind for help and find ourselves dreaming about pedantic attitudes.

To understand body puns and illnesses in dreams, it is probably easiest to start by dividing the body into recognized systems, since so often the problem is a symptom of something happening elsewhere. For example, varicose veins in the legs are actually a problem with the circulatory system. The main systems are the circulatory system; the digestive system; the endocrine system; the nervous system; the reproductive system; the respiratory system; the urinary system; and the skeleton, muscles and skin.

This chapter contains a brief description of each system, together with its more common problems and their generally accepted meanings. This is followed by a list of common metaphors connected with each system. Reading through these lists can indicate some disruption in your life related to a physical problem. When you find a suitable metaphor, or even think of one yourself, use this to incubate a dream.

The Circulatory System

This is the system which circulates the blood around the body, providing nourishment and oxygen and eliminating waste products. It also maintains the body at an even temperature. Blood is composed of plasma, red and white corpuscles (cells) and platelets. Plasma is the straw-coloured fluid in which the cells and platelets float. As it circulates, it carries nourishment and collects waste, which is then passed to the kidneys for excretion. The red cells carry oxygen from the lungs to the tissues throughout the body. They then collect carbon dioxide, carrying it to the lungs for exhalation. They also carry haemoglobin, a shortage of which can result in anaemia. The white cells are the defence mechanism for destroying disease. The platelets cause the blood to clot.

Blood is generally classified in four major groups known as A, B, AB and O. There is also another blood group system, the Rhesus factor (RH factor), which is taken into account in pregnancy. Blood is pumped around the body by the heart through arteries, veins and capillaries. These pathways need to remain clear to maintain good health and avoid excessive stress on the heart. Furring up of arteries due to bad diet and lack of exercise leads to many heart problems. A blood pressure reading is the speed of the pumping heart in relation to the pressure needed to force the blood through the valves and around the system.

There is also a secondary circulatory system, known as the lymphatic system. This returns excess fluid from the tissues back into the main circulatory system. The lymph vessels have a similar structure to veins and contain valves. The fluid is moved through pressure on the muscles during exercise. Blockages lead to swelling.

Problems
Congestive heart failure; coronary thrombosis; stroke; embolism; high blood pressure; anaemia; aneurysm; angina; atherosclerosis; haemophilia; gangrene; chilblains; oedema; palpitations; phlebitis; varicose veins.

Meanings
Most commonly love and emotions; being at the centre of things; feeling under pressure; life force.

Metaphors
To be at the heart of things; to take heart; to break your heart; wearing your heart on your sleeve; eating your heart out; doing

something to your heart's content; taking things to heart; having your heart in your mouth; being heart-broken; being heartless; heart-searching; pulling at your heart-strings; having a heart-to-heart; heart-rending. It's in your blood; making your blood boil; in cold blood; blood is thicker than water; making your blood run cold; bloodbath; blood-curdling; blood and thunder; blood brother; blood money; bloodline; bloodsucker; blood-thirsty.

The Digestive System

Before food can be absorbed into the body it has to be digested. Firstly, it is reduced to a pulp in the mouth through being chewed and mixed with saliva. Then it is swallowed down the oesophagus into the stomach. Here it meets the gastric juices which further break it down. Some liquids are absorbed through the stomach walls at this stage. The remainder continues into the carefully folded 20-foot long small intestine. At this point fluids from the liver and pancreas continue the process of extracting nutrients from the food. The function of the liver is the manufacture of bile. This contains bile salts which help with the emulsification of fats. The liver also removes excess amino acids by converting them into urea. It is the body's main detoxifier for poisonous substances such as alcohol and drugs. It converts fat and creates heat.

Finally, the indigestible matter proceeds to the large intestine and down into the bowels where it is eliminated through the anus. The movement process is known as peristalsis.

Problems
Anorexia; bulimia; indigestion; vomiting; duodenal ulcer; gastritis; hiatus hernia; nausea; peptic ulcers; travel sickness; appendicitis; liver cirrhosis; constipation; cancer; diarrhoea; flatulence; diverticulosis; gallstones; hepatitis; irritable bowel syndrome; jaundice; peritonitis; pancreatitis; haemorrhoids; bladder problems; cystitis; incontinence; kidney stones; pyelonephritis.

Meanings
Assimilation; elimination; hunger; craving; comfort eating; sensitivity and feelings; rejection; digestion; loss of control; excessive control; tension; vulnerability.

Metaphors
Eating your words; eating your heart out; food for thought; having a gut feeling; having the guts to do something; stomaching something; can't stomach it; butterflies in the stomach; digesting information; having a lot of gall; what is eating you?; having a lot of spleen; relieving yourself; unloading yourself; being liverish.

The Endocrine System

The endocrine system controls the metabolism. It co-ordinates the long-term body functions such as growth, parallel to the nervous system which deals more with the short-term. It consists of a number of hormone-producing ductless glands, which respond to stimulation through the senses, emotions and chemicals in the body. The hypothalamus at the base of the forebrain is the prime mover, while the pituitary gland in the head is the overall manager. It produces a number of hormones which stimulate the other endocrine glands. It controls the water levels in the body and affects growth. The thyroid gland is found in the throat and affects energy levels. Its hormone stimulates the metabolism and is essential for growth in children. Deficiencies respond to iodine. The adrenal glands lie just above the kidneys. They control the 'fight or flight' reflex in response to stimulation from the sympathetic nervous system, giving a rush of adrenaline in times of stress and fear. The islets of Langerhans are found in the pancreas near the spleen. They produce insulin which is responsible for the control of glucose. Problems in this area give rise to diabetes. Finally there are the testes in men, producing testosterone for the production of sperm and for sexual development, and the ovaries in women, producing oestrogen for maintaining female characteristics.

Problems
Addison's disease; bulging eyes; Cushing's syndrome; diabetes; growth problems; goitre; gout; hypoglycaemia; obesity; thyroid problems; weight loss; hormone imbalance.

Meanings
Balance; co-ordination; obsession; self-indulgence.

Metaphors
Getting a rush of adrenaline; taking a balanced view.

The Nervous System

The nervous system is the body's communication network. It operates from the brain, down the spinal cord and out into the nerve fibres all over the body. It is in two parts. Firstly there is the central nervous system which governs the senses and reactions. It comprises sensory nerves which inform the brain, and motor nerves which control actions and reactions. Alongside this is the autonomic nervous system which is self-governing. It controls all the automatic processes in the body. It is made up of two parts. The sympathetic system stimulates organs concerned with immediate activity. When we are afraid, for example, it speeds up the heartbeat, accelerates the breathing and diverts the necessary chemicals which enable us to run away. The parasympathetic system is the one that keeps us alive. It is our automatic pilot that keeps everything going when we are asleep.

Problems
Bell's palsy; brain injury; dizziness; encephalitis; epilepsy; fainting; fits; headaches; migraine; multiple sclerosis; numbness; paralysis; Parkinson's disease; polio; stroke; all nervous disorders such as depression, bruxism, addictions, anorexia, bulimia, grief, shock, hypochondria, obsessions, paranoia, phobias and insomnia.

Meanings
Sensitivity; intercommunication; wiring and circuits; breakdowns; lassitude and idleness.

Metaphors
Having something on the brain; picking someone's brains; racking your brains; having a brainchild; the brain drain; he's completely brain-dead; simply brainless; he's got to be brain-sick; brainstorming; brain-teaser; being brainwashed; he gets on my nerves; he's got a nerve; being in the nerve centre; being completely nerveless; finding things nerve-racking.

The Reproductive System

The reproductive system is designed for procreation. The male's is on the outside of the body and consists of the scrotum, containing the sperm-producing testes, and the penis. The female's organs are internal and consist of the uterus, ovaries and fallopian tubes. Oestrogen is produced in the ovaries which releases the egg into the uterus where it can be fertilized or excreted monthly if unfertilized.

Problems
In men – cancer; prostate difficulties; cryptorchidism; impotence; lack of erection; warts. In women – amenorrhoea; dysmenorrhoea; menorrhagia; cancer; cysts; fibroids; endometriosis; hysterectomy; menopause; menstrual problems; PMT; vaginal and vulval problems; warts. Sexually transmitted diseases occur in both sexes.

Meanings
Sexual desires; passion; creative desires; self-abuse; domination versus inability; emotional blockages. The womb often represents fertility; creativity; sowing seeds; retreat to the foetal state; fear and insecurity; disintegration then re-integration.

Metaphors
Since most of these are impolite you will need to look for your own associations!

The Respiratory System

The lungs work like a pair of bellows through the action of an arched muscle called the diaphragm which is under the control of the autonomic nervous system. Respiration takes place through the inhalation of air into the nose, and down the trachea which divides into tubes called bronchi which in turn lead into the two lungs. Here the bronchi split into myriads of fine branches or bronchioles which end in alveoli or airsacs. Oxygen is extracted from the air and passes into the bloodstream through the thin walls of the airsacs. The blood returns it used as carbon dioxide which passes back the same way to be exhaled through the bronchi and trachea. The walls of the airways keep the lungs moist through the production of mucus. They are also covered with tiny hairs to trap dust and pollen and other foreign bodies, keeping the lungs clear. We normally breathe about 16 times a minute. This increases under stimulation such as running. The healthier you are, the slower you breathe.

Problems
Asthma; pulmonary oedema; breathlessness; bronchitis; cancer; chest pains; cough; emphysema; hiccups; pleurisy; pneumonia; tuberculosis.

Meanings
Feelings; emotions; secret longings; hopes; sensitivity; receptiveness; nurturing.

Metaphors
Catching your breath; holding your breath; saving your breath; taking your breath away; in the same breath; under your

breath; taking a deep breath; taking a breather; finding a breathing space; it's simply breath-taking; having a breath test.

The Urinary System

This system works through the kidneys, a pair of bean-shaped organs situated between the muscles of the lower back and the digestive organs. Urea is the waste that collects in the liver and is then passed on to the kidneys. The kidneys expel urine which is a mixture of water and urea. The urine flows along ureters into the bladder which contracts when full, excreting the urine through the urethra.

Problems
Bladder control; bladder stones; cystitis; Bright's disease; incontinence; kidney failure; painful urination; retention of urine.

Meanings
Relieving yourself of unwanted waste; releasing your hold; stop clinging on; loss of emotional control; filtering; cleansing.

Metaphors
Laughing till you wet yourself; taking the piss; being pissed off; piss off; pissing on; being pissed; being a piss artist; being peed on; relieving yourself; what a relief.

The Skeleton, Muscles and Skin

These represent the main structure of the body. The skeleton is the frame on which everything else is built. The muscles hold the body together and the skin encloses it, allowing it to breathe and helping to control its temperature.

Problems
Fractures; ossification; osteoporosis; sprains; strains; ruptures; arthritis; rheumatism; bursitis; cramp; hernia; lumbago;

osteoarthritis; slipped disc; sciatica; tendonitis; rashes; acne; flushes; psoriasis.

Meanings
The skeleton and muscles are almost entirely to do with frame-work and support, and also connections and mobility. Strain and breakdown mean a need to ease off and rest, usually because previous signals have been ignored. The skin is connected with our overall protection or vulnerability. Blushing represents shyness, while birthmarks can represent stains on our character.

Metaphors
Many of the metaphors relating to the back apply here: muscling in; being muscle-bound; being skinned alive; having a tough skin; having a thick skin; by the skin of your teeth; getting under one's skin; jumping out of your skin; no skin off your nose; saving your skin; only skin-deep; a skinhead; a skinflint; having a skinful; skin-tight.

Now that you have had a chance to examine the possibilities of these metaphors, think about how you use language. People who talk about being 'pissed off' frequently have urinary problems. How about 'it makes my blood boil'? Do you easily get red in the face, blush or have palpitations? Think of the body-related expressions that you use most frequently and then explore them in your dreams.

9

· ·

Understanding Our Dreams (2)– The Imagery of the Body

Individual body parts and associated language can be focused on in the same way to reveal aspects of ourselves. Many of these words and phrases will be used by the dream mind in a picture form or will stimulate connected memories, according to your early personal experience. Again, only the more common problems have been listed here. Look through the following meanings and metaphors and try to find a seed thought for a dream.

HAIR

Problems

Greasy; lank; split ends; falling out; balding; going grey/white.

Meanings

Hair symbolizes strength and thoughts and ideas. When it is hanging loose it reflects youth and freedom, whereas when it is plaited or bound it refers to the restrictions of maturity or subjugation. Cutting or losing hair can mean your strength or energy levels are being reduced. Alternatively, it might mean improving your view of things. Hair standing on end indicates shock or fear. Balding can be equated with tonsures, suggesting a desire to contact higher levels. Tangled hair shows confusion. Greying hair can mean stress as well as ageing. Wigs and hairpieces indicate that all is not as it seems, and that there is a cover-up.

Metaphors

Get in someone's hair; get out of your hair; let your hair down; to split hairs; without turning a hair; to win by a hair's breadth; wearing a hair shirt; hair doesn't grow on a busy street; baldy; hairy; a hairy adventure; hair-raising.

THE HEAD

Problems
Headaches; migraine; concussion; dizziness; fainting; fits; woolly thinking.

Meanings
The head represents the mind, analysis, wisdom, ideas, logic, mental powers, leadership, contact with higher levels, a source, a scheme or a plot. It is mainly about being on top or in front, leading a group, holding your head up high or bowing down before others. It can also mean getting to the source of things, as in the head of a river or bringing things to a head. It is also about succeeding.

Metaphors
Holding your head up high; getting your head down; losing your head; heading the ball; making headway; putting your heads together; to have your head turned; bringing things to a head; being head-hunted; having a head start; running round like a headless chicken; being scalped; feeling heady; dizzy-headed; biting someone's head off; going to your head; keeping your head above water; head and shoulders above the rest; taking it into your head; cannot make head nor tail of it; off the top of your head; off or out of your head; everything goes over my head; going in head-first; a screw loose; a head case; not all there; dealing with things head-on; being head over heels. There are very many other expressions.

THE FACE

Problems
Acne; spots; wrinkles; birthmarks; distortions; large features; facial hair.

Meaning
The face can be our own appearance or recognition of others. It is the image that we present to the world. Frequently we hide

our true selves. This could appear as a painted face or a mask. Faceless images can mean you have lost face, but can also indicate our special guides. A face can mean the courage to face up to things.

Metaphors

Facing up to things; losing face; coming face to face; facing facts; laughing in your face; in the face of; fly in the face of; pulling faces; setting your face against; showing your face; saying it to someone's face; turning face down; face-saving; taking things at face value; being self-effacing.

THE EYES

Problems

Blindness; myopia; watering; styes; allergy; cataract; glaucoma; astigmatism; cross-eyed; lazy eye.

Meaning

Eyes are to do with seeing or a refusal to see something. They are known as the windows of the soul. They are about clarity and being willing to see or conversely about being blind. There is also the third eye or single eye, the source of intuition and awareness. Eyes are also about watchfulness, expression and crying. There is also the fear of the dark and not being able to see. You can be forced to look or not allowed to see. 'There are none so blind as those who do not want to see.' Spectacles also come into this category.

Metaphors

The mote in your eye; keeping an eye on things; the glad eye; the evil eye; looking through rose-coloured spectacles; an eye for an eye; a black eye; the all-seeing eye; through the eye of a needle; four-eyes; the apple of my eye; to be all eyes; catching someone's eye; having an eye for; being in the public eye; being in the eye of the wind; keeping your eyes peeled; the whites of the eyes; a sight for sore eyes; seeing eye to eye; being up to your eyes; an eye-catcher; far-sighted; near-sighted; cross-eyed; inability to see what's under your nose.

THE EARS

Problems
Deafness; tinnitus; glue ear; ruptured eardrum; earache; blocked Eustachian tubes; selective hearing.

Meaning
Ears are about being willing to hear, listen and co-operate. They are also about deafness and lack of understanding or an unwillingness to hear the truth. Everything connected with sound should be considered in this context, together with an understanding of selective hearing. 'There are none so deaf as those who do not want to hear.'

Metaphors
Hear, hear!; keeping your ear to the ground; keeping your ears open; turning a deaf ear; being all ears; getting one by the ears; having the ear of someone; going in one ear and out the other; playing by ear; up to your ears; wet behind the ears; earmarking something; with a flea in their ear; even the walls have ears.

THE NOSE

Problems
Stuffy nose; large nose; sinusitis; loss of smell; sneezing; catarrh; hayfever; broken nose; nosebleeds; snoring.

Meaning
Noses are to do with breathing, smelling, loss of smell or something 'getting up your nose'. Other associations include nosiness, inquisitiveness, curiosity and knowingness. The nose represents intuition and instincts. It can also mean telling falsehoods (eg Pinnochio).

Metaphors

Poking your nose in; having your nose put out of joint; having a nose for it; a nosy Parker; cutting off your nose to spite your face; paying through the nose; plain as the nose on your face; nose to the grindstone; led by the nose; following your nose; keeping your nose clean; looking down your nose; turning up your nose; nosing out; making a nose dive; thumbing your nose; getting up your nose. Also in this category are expressions to do with good and bad smells, and the irritations of snoring.

THE MOUTH

Problems

Sore lips; cold sores; swollen tongue; ulcers; halitosis/bad breath; laryngitis; sore throat; tonsilitis; loss of voice; stuttering/stammering.

Meanings

The mouth is to do with taste, eating, swallowing, starving and dieting. It is also connected with communication, silence, talking too much, being a gossip, being obsequious, being aggressive or being dumb. It can be about paying lip service or having a stiff upper lip. The lips and tongue relate closely to words and articulation, and also to the intimacy of kissing

Metaphors

Being a dumb-cluck; being a dumb blonde; being dumbfounded or dumbstruck; having verbal diarrhoea; paying lip service; stiff upper lip; giving a bit of lip; biting your lip; on the tip of your tongue; giving tongue; holding your tongue; a sharp tongue; tongue-in-cheek; tongue-tied; keeping your mouth shut; giving a tongue-lashing; being down in the mouth; shooting your mouth off; shut your mouth; being mouthy; something mouth-watering; jumping down your throat; sticking in your throat; the voice of experience; having no voice of your own; speaking with one voice; speaking volumes.

TEETH

Problems
Toothache; infections; rotting teeth; loose teeth; false teeth; extractions; crooked teeth; impacted teeth; braces; bruxism; mercury poisoning; gingivitis; gumboils; dentures.

Meaning
Teeth are connected with biting, chewing or grinding, or getting something stuck in your teeth. They can mean indecisiveness. They are also about maturity – losing baby teeth and growing second teeth or wisdom teeth. When the teeth are loose or falling out it can mean talking too much and giving away secrets, or simply old age. They are about words – good, bad or false.

Metaphors
Long in the tooth; fighting tooth and nail; fed up to the back teeth; toothsome; getting your teeth into something; giving your eye teeth for something; being in the teeth of something; getting a kick in the teeth; lying in your teeth; setting your teeth on edge; showing your teeth; armed to the teeth; biting on a problem; biting the bullet; speaking bitingly; something is beginning to bite; biting back your words; putting the bite on something; the biter bit; chewing the fat; chewing on a problem; to chew over; to chew up.

THE NECK

Problems
Stiffness; whiplash injuries; pulled muscles; disc problems; cervical spondylosis; headaches; meningitis.

Meaning
The neck supports the head and enables one to look in several directions and hence to see both sides of something. It also shows our levels of pride, flexibility or submissiveness. It can also be about kissing (necking).

Metaphors
Being stiff-necked; a pain in the neck; sticking your neck out; risking your neck; getting it in the neck; going neck and neck; going all out to break your neck; in your neck of the woods; the neck of the channel.

THE SHOULDERS

Problems
Frozen shoulder; dislocation; fractures; pulled muscles; joint injury.

Meaning
Shoulders are about carrying, lifting, supporting and caring.

Metaphors
Shouldering responsibilities; a shoulder to lean on; putting one's shoulder to the wheel; rubbing shoulders with; standing shoulder to shoulder; straight from the shoulder; having a shoulder to cry on; shouldering the burdens of others.

THE ARMS AND ELBOWS

Problems
Sprains and fractures; referred pains (cervical or angina); tendonitis; tennis elbow; bursitis; dislocations.

Meanings
Arms represent an ability to grasp and reach out. They are for carrying, caring, hugging, supplication, surrendering, praying, embracing or protection. They are also about weapons and defence.

Metaphors
Going arm-in-arm; keeping something at arm's length; with open arms; twisting your arm; bearing arms; under arms; shouldering arms; laying down your arms; up in arms; up to your elbows; elbowed out of the way; elbow grease; making elbow room.

THE HANDS

Problems
Carpal tunnel syndrome; swelling; arthritis; stiffness.

Meaning
Hands usually indicate service, work, giving and taking, touch and feeling, praying, pleading or applauding. They can relate to the directions of left and right. Fingers indicate dexterity and power.

Metaphors
Open-handed; giving a hand; can or can't handle it; giving a hand-out; being on hand; changing hands; forcing someone's hand; being hand-in-glove; having your hands full; keeping your hand in; out of hand; playing into the hands of someone; taking in hand; throwing up your hands; washing your hands of something; heavy-handed; a handful; cack-handed; a hand-me-down; living hand-to-mouth; to hand pick; to be hands-on; second-hand; pointing a finger; burning your fingers; having a finger on something; having a finger in the pie; twisting someone around your little finger; pulling your finger out; snapping your fingers; having it at your fingertips; getting the thumbs-up.

THE BACK

Problems
Damaged back; fibrositis; pulled muscles; sprains; slipped discs; spondylitis; curvature of the spine; sciatica; strain of the sacroiliac joint; rheumatoid arthritis.

Meaning
The back is to do with strength, support, uprightness, responsibility, carrying burdens and having backbone.

Metaphors
Feeling unsupported; having backbone; turning your back; revealing your back; someone on your back; a pain in the

back; the last straw that breaks the camel's back; putting your back into something; get off your back; behind someone's back; doing something back-to-front; stabbing someone in the back; having your back to the wall; getting someone's back up; backing down; backing up; backing off; backing out; going back on; being a back-biter; putting something on the back-boiler; finding something back-breaking; coming in through the back door; back-dating something; something has backfired; giving a back-hander; being in the backseat.

THE LEGS AND KNEES

Problems

Swollen legs and joints; pulled muscles; fractures; dislocations; varicose veins; cramps; deep vein thrombosis; DVT; thrombophlebitis.

Meaning

Legs are about support, having a leg to stand on and mobility. They are about agility and strength. Being weak at the knees shows fear and a lack of courage. Kneeling is about respect or supplication.

Metaphors

Not having a leg to stand on; a leg-up; making a stand; taking a stance; on your last legs; showing a leg; shaking a leg; pulling someone's leg; stretching your legs; being legless; being a leg-man; doing the legwork; having plenty of leg-room; taking a stand; taking the stand; standing up to; standing up for; standing down; standing for; just standing by; standing by someone; on standby; being a stand-in; having good standing; standing off (as in a ship); being in a stand-off; being brought to your knees; kneeling in awe or submission; being kneecapped; knee-high to a grasshopper; a knee-jerk reaction; a knees-up; getting down on your knees; going down on one knee.

THE FEET

Problems
Flat feet; fallen arches; burning feet; bunions; corns and calluses; verrucas and warts; athlete's foot; sprains; swollen feet; difficulty in walking.

Meaning
Feet are about our foundations, being grounded, courage, walking, taking the first step and self-propulsion. Heels can be a pun representing healing, but heels and Achilles tendons are also weak spots. Heeling can also mean tipping sideways, as in sailing. Toes are about our personal position. Remember also the Footsie – the FT Financial Index (FTSE).

Metaphors
Putting your best foot forward; putting your foot down; getting cold feet; caught on the wrong foot or wrong-footed; not putting a foot wrong; putting your foot in it; getting underfoot; one foot in the grave; having a foothold; getting a footing; following in someone's footsteps; going barefoot; being footloose and fancy-free; falling on your feet; keeping both feet on the ground; feet of clay; rushed off your feet; standing on your own two feet; being swept off your feet; finding your feet; voting with your feet; digging your heels in; cooling your heels; being down-at-heel; taking to your heels; laid by the heels; showing a clean pair of heels; under the heel of someone; the heel of your hand; being a heel; brought to heel; on one's toes; getting a toe-hold; treading on someone's toes; toeing the line; being a toe-rag.

If metaphors such as these occur in dreams and are related to bodily complaints, we need to look at our lifestyle. In dream healing, we deal with the whole person and not just isolated parts. Once the context is understood, these expressions can reveal how much we become victims of circumstances.

10

•••••••••••••••••••••••

Understanding Our Dreams (3) – Important Dream Symbols

The Four Elements

The human body is said to be 80 per cent water, plus earth (skin and bone), fire (body warmth) and air (the breath). If any of these four elements appears in our dreams, it can have very definite connections with our health.

This fourfold balance was highlighted by Hippocrates (460 BC), the father of medicine, who considered the body to consist of the four humours: blood, phlegm, black bile and yellow bile. These later became known as 'temperaments' and were named sanguine, phlegmatic, melancholic and choleric. Michael Scott (c1175 AD), a Scottish scholar known as the 'wondrous wizard', who translated the works of Aristotle, was apparently the first person to connect these humours with dreams. He specialized in astrology and incorporated the date, time and place of birth of an individual, together with the positions of the planets, into dream interpretation. He thought that dreams were diagnostic of physical illnesses, which were caused by imbalances between the four humours or conditions of dryness, humidity, hot and cold.

The names of these humours are still used in our general language to illustrate certain behavioural patterns. Sanguine/blood is usually equated with the element of air. Sanguine people are usually wise, passionate, cheerful and courageous. They can also be weak and given to sudden changes of mood. Phlegmatic/phlegm is the element of water. These people are calm and strong but lacking in vivacity. They tend to be sluggish but find their own level. Melancholic/black bile is the element of earth. These people are dependable, stable and solid but given to being depressed and gloomy. Choleric/yellow bile is the element of fire. Choleric people are often aggressive, sharp, creative and emotionally strong, but can sometimes be irritable and angry. In our dreams, therefore, we need to be aware of any elemental dominance – water, earth, air or fire.

Water

If we are in a state of great sluggishness or if we are dehydrated or suffering from fluid retention, oedema or urinary trouble, we need to consider the element of water.

Water relates to our emotions, sensuality and sexuality, and the unconscious mind. Water can be expansive and calm, cold and forbidding, muddy and unpleasant, slimy, hot, flowing or ice-bound, to mention a few ideas. You may want to throw off your clothes and bathe in it, dabble your hands in it, paddle, or go nowhere near it. It may be in the form of a lake, a pool, a river, a trough, a puddle, a bucket or a sink.

So if your dream contains rivers, lakes, oceans, swamps, marshes, quicksands, floods, tidal waves, beaches, ice, and so on, you can be sure that something profound is going on for you. The condition of the water provides clues to the state of your emotions (stormy, muddy, fast moving, sluggish, still, clear, windswept, frozen, and so on). If something is crawling out of the water or emerging from the depths, then something that has been repressed on an emotional level is surfacing. The greater the depth, the longer the repression and the greater the release.

Perhaps one of the water-related systems is causing you trouble (*see* Chapter 8). It could be the urinary system, the respiratory system (connected with mucus), or alternatively the reproductive system. Remember that repressed emotions can lead to physical difficulties.

I am standing by a small powerful river with a bridge over it. I am apprehensive about crossing. On the left the flow is intense and on the right there is a sheer drop. Suddenly there is a great torrent which takes a wall with it. Then everything is peaceful and the remains of the wall offer a safe passage over the water.

• •

This dream suggests that there are strong emotions which need to be released before a gap can be safely bridged. The dreamer needs to allow the flood to take place and let things be destroyed in the process. This dream could be to do with a fear of heights, dizziness or a problem with the ears. The dreamer could either be overwhelmed by noise or refusing to hear, but either way the dam will burst. The dream could also relate to some form of festering such as a boil or ulcers.

Beaches are interesting since they are a combination of land and sea (earth/water). They are, therefore, transitional. They are places where slates are washed clean and we can make a fresh start. Tidal waves rarely drown us but rather show that we will survive immense emotional upheavals. Pools or bowls of water have profound meanings, firstly because they are usually still, and we can often see the bottom and what, if anything, is rising, and secondly because they reflect. Wells and oases are interesting because they indicate refreshment when in need. However, they can also represent pollution, entrapment or stagnant situations.

Earth

Depression, insecurity, or trouble with support or foundations (legs, feet or back) mean that we need to look to earth. This element frequently dominates dreams and is to do with stability and strength. We dream of mountains, valleys, fields, hills, moors, tundra, steppes, plains, woodland, deserts or jungle, but what is important is how they are presented. Is your dreamscape bleak, cold, deserted, warm, inviting, a struggle to get through, cultivated, rich? Are you constantly going uphill – having a tough time; downhill – on a slippery slope; hidden from the sun or being roasted; caught in an earthquake? The earth element gives clear indications of our sense of security.

Dreaming of being in a jungle and apparently flying just above marshy ground, for example, suggests that life has been rather like a jungle recently. The fact that the dreamer is flying shows that he is now releasing himself from what has been impenetrable and holding him back. The dream is saying it is time to confront the jungle of ideas about his health. Instead of getting emotional, the dreamer needs to rise above the situation and visit the doctor.

Air

Dreaming of air represents passion, courage and communication. Are you feeling weak with no get-up-and-go, or do you have problems with breathing, with the throat and lungs?

Air is more difficult to define because we can only see, feel and hear its effects. We cannot see it for itself. In the main, we associate air with the sky and clouds. It is connected with communication so it relates to how we put ourselves across. Air can be represented by anything from a breeze to a full-blown hurricane or tornado. Be aware of how it feels and the sound it makes, as this could be telling you something really important. Messages are carried on the wind.

One dreamer described dreaming of returning to her father's windmill in Poland. Inside there were several men sitting near the walls. In this dream the windmill indicates the element of air. The men represent elders, the source of wisdom. As windmills nowadays tend to be non-functional, the dreamer needs to check her lungs and breathing and ask advice from her elders.

Fire

When anger, irritability and generally explosive feelings dominate, perhaps with upset stomachs, fire/change is the key.

Fire manifests in dreams in many ways and relates to creativity and transformation. Whatever is touched by fire has its form permanently changed. It can never be the same again, but is reborn like the phoenix out of the ashes. In the dreamscape, fire is represented by deserts, volcanoes, forest fires, bonfires, beacons, campfires and burning buildings, and in dreams of the home it can appear as hearth fires, central heating, electricity, gas, electric blankets and other appliances, candles or matches. Its energy can vary from gentle warmth to smoking, smouldering, erupting, raging or exploding. When fire appears in your dreams, be conscious of extra energy or of change.

I went into a flower shop and bought a flower arrangement with a lace-covered baby's crib in it. Suddenly the crib burst into flames and the shop assistant said it was the wrong time of the year to light it. The baby died.

Flowers are to do with hope and promises for the future, so the 'baby' (the dreamer's creation) should develop into something important. However, it needs to be transformed first to make it viable. Also, something needs checking in the reproductive area before it flares up.

Time

Time plays an important part in our dreams since all of life is cyclical. We need, therefore, to explore time correspondences since they can have very powerful associations. Most dreams tend to take place in the present or in no apparent time phase. However, any dream that goes back in time relates to past experience. If we dream of childhood, of grandparents or of ancestors, we need to examine the facts within the context of the past. Similarly, dreams which appear to relate to the future or to space travel can be precognitive. Dreams of time can also indicate that it is time to stop procrastinating.

Day and night, dawn and dusk, midnight and noon – each have a profound significance. We have built-in reactions to each period of the day, so we need to look at both expected behaviour and our individual behaviour. The lark is a very different creature from the night owl, and their dreams can have very different interpretations.

The same applies to the seasons of the year. Spring is a time of stirring and awakening and equates with childhood; summer a time of attraction and luxuriant growth, equating with youth;

autumn is the time of fruition and harvest, and is connected with maturity; winter is the time of retreat, rest and old age. Seasonal festivals have been celebrated since time immemorial and are based on the cycles of the sun. In the dream world, recognizing these natural timescales can help tremendously with pacing ourselves in our waking lives.

We can also take into account the weather patterns in connection with the time cycles. If in a dream it is obviously high summer and we are in a snow storm, the situation could be quite tricky. In the same way, intense heat during the resting time of winter could lead to unnatural growth. These somewhat bizarre images can tell us a lot about ourselves.

Weather conditions – calm, cloudy, hot, cold, gloomy, threatening, stormy, foggy, and so on – can mirror, through association, what is happening currently in our lives and what to be wary of. Checking your dream journal for patterns can reveal how you respond to weather. Many of us become overwhelmed with gloom when the sky is overcast, especially if the cloud is persistent over several days. There is also Seasonal Affective Disorder (SAD) which afflicts so many of us as the days grow shorter and we are starved of daylight. Unrelenting sunshine and heat also create oppression.

Death, Killings and Burials

Death dreams can be precognitive, but this is very rare. There are also instances where people have dreamed of their own deaths. The general view here is that such an intuition is a form of preparation for the event. It enables the dreamer to come to terms with the tragedy, to be strong and help others through the crisis.

The more common meaning of dreaming about death is the end of something, something that has run its course and is ready to die and be buried. This can apply to people, situations, habits or strong beliefs. In a healing context, it could be showing that belief in an out-dated treatment is inhibiting the healing process.

Death dreams can manifest in a number of ways. Perhaps we see someone dead or see our own death, or we are killing or being killed, or we are at the burial or funeral of another, or we are at our own funeral, or we are in a graveyard. In each case the message is the same. It is a time of release and new beginnings. It can also mean that we are wishing someone dead or we would like to kill them off, bury them and get them out of our sight. So when considering the meaning of death dreams, it is important to know whether the dead person is ourself or someone else.

Ritual sacrifice or torture can be a clear mirror of our waking life. We may be depressed and unhappy and unable to understand why. Such dreams help us to recognize the situation and identify our problem. This could be calling our attention to some sort of self-inflicted illness such as the results of smoking or over-eating.

Babies

In dreams babies usually have an entirely different meaning from the obvious. However, it is always wise to consider them literally first of all. Have you a need to return to the foetal? Do you feel like a helpless baby? If you have an illness that resembles some sort of childhood disease, this can bring on baby dreams.

The more general interpretation is that they represent our ideas, our latent talents and our creations. They are things that we have conceived and either do or do not give birth to or allow to develop. Often in our dreams, something terrible happens to the baby. We lose it, throw it out with the bath water, or give it away, meaning that we have neglected our abilities in some way.

These dreams can also indicate missing the point of an incubated dream. The dreamer has asked for a solution and has either disregarded or dismissed the answer.

I am going somewhere on a bike with a small baby which is totally neglected and uncared for. I just about manage to feed it. The way is narrow, uphill and hard to find, but I am determined to get there.

The dreamer here has obviously been neglecting his talents whilst struggling up a hard and narrow route. What is being shown here is that determination will win the day, no matter how hard life may appear to be at present. The important thing is to continue to nurture hopes.

There are occasions when we feel that someone has stolen, or is about to steal, our ideas. This happens much more frequently than we realize, but it is not lost on the dream mind. In such a case we may dream about losing a child, or about unpleasant characters lurking around the child. This shows how valuable dreaming can be in helping us not to miss opportunities.

Dreams of pregnancy indicate that something is gestating. We have sown seeds and conceived and are now given the responsibility of bringing things to fruition. An easy pregnancy augurs well, while a difficult one shows either reluctance or a lot of problems along the way. Again these dreams can be associated with dream incubation, so we need to interpret them on both levels – as an advice dream or an answer to our seeding.

Births speak for themselves and show that your idea has reached the light of day and now needs nurturing. Again births can be easy or difficult. Dreams of still births or abortions show that you have allowed your idea or talent to die or have decided to abandon it before it has come to full term. They can also represent miscarriages of justice.

Sex

Sexual dreams can improve our sex lives. If in your dreams you have the most amazing erotic experiences yet your ordinary life seems dull and mechanical, it could be that you set the wrong scenario for yourself in reality. If you are keeping a record of your dreams, you can look for the patterns.

These dreams are clear messages from our unconscious minds. Because of this we need to be aware of the images and symbols, which also frequent our waking lives. Virtually all rigid pointed objects, such as a poker, are phallic, particularly if they are being inserted into an opening or crevice. Keys come into this category, but usually have a more profound meaning. The Key is a source of currently needed information. If it is a house key does it take you into the hall (a place of transit) or into the kitchen (a place of nourishment)? If it is a car key, you need to make a journey – the information is somewhere else. Keys to cellars or dungeons indicate a need to explore what you are suppressing. Cupboard keys ask what is hidden in the cupboard; keys to jewel boxes mean that there is something valuable to be found. Old keys usually mean that you have been a long time becoming aware of the need to explore the locks in yourself; new ones usually show action is in the present.

Tools bring an immediate response since we use the word anyway as a phallic symbol. Thus screwdrivers, drills, pile drivers, hammers and nails all have double meanings. Weapons – rifles, swords, daggers – all show that domination is in mind. How about bananas, dipsticks or rockets and space shuttles?

We should also look at wilting or flexible objects. Balloons that won't inflate, a limp garden hose, a drooping flower, a damp squib or even a jack-in-a-box with a broken spring can all indicate our fears of inadequacy and can apply equally to men and women. Other powerful images are, of course, beds and bedrooms, cocks, seeds and especially motor cars, which in dreams are images of ourselves. The fast sports car can be under or out of control. It can also refuse to start or run out of fuel. The female is often represented by a hole of some sort, an entrance or a ring. Sometimes these entrances are blocked, which speaks for itself. Apples, melons, cows, nuts – these words are all part of our everyday vocabulary, so the clues are there.

A man dreams of a smouldering fire. He picks up an old-fashioned poker and starts to encourage the flames. Quickly the fire takes hold but he pokes it so violently that the coals fall out and burn him. He finds a bucket of water and douses the flames. This dream shows that at some time in the past, he deliberately stirred up a sexual passion, only to discover that he could not handle it. Because burns scar, he is still carrying the guilt. Dousing the fire shows that he can be in control.

Sex is often described as 'a fire in the belly' and lovers are 'old flames'. Consider also the expressions like 'he turns me on/off' – we might dream of a tap that runs dry, since water is connected with the emotions.

Rabbits, snakes, bulls, wolves and unicorns are frequently sexual symbols. Rabbits because they are so fertile, snakes because of their resemblance to spermatozoa, bulls for their virility and unicorns for their horns. Of course, we are all familiar with the reputation of the wolf.

A woman dreams she is with her boyfriend in a holiday cottage that is losing its walls. Suddenly a magnificent unicorn appears. Its horn curves downwards. It charges the house, breathing rage. The boyfriend runs, while she kneels before the unicorn. It is sunset. This dream shows her in a temporary refuge which is falling apart. The unicorn represents her sexual needs, and when it charges it frightens her boyfriend, whereas she submits to it. The sunset shows the relationship is at an end.

In another dream scenario, a woman sees sheep being attacked by a wolf and the farmer sends hounds to kill it. The wolf crawls near the dreamer on a ledge, its skin flayed off. She becomes a hound, then human again. The ledge is precarious and made of novels and some skirts. She knows she is going to fall. This suggests that someone she cares for has earned a wolf reputation and is being harassed by colleagues. She also becomes an accessory to his downfall. Not being entirely innocent, she finds herself in a precarious position with him. The feeling that she will fall shows that she will have to confess. Her life is based on ideas in romantic novels and losing her skirts can mean sexual desire. This shows a need for excitement combined with guilt.

In the dream state it is perfectly normal for men to have erections and women to become moist as erotic images titillate our senses. They are far more exciting than porn or blue films because we actually take part. Lots of dreamers find this desperately embarrassing, but this is just the dream mind showing us that we are not impotent or frigid. The problem is that in everyday life our partners simply do not turn us on.

Some people never have a satisfactory love life in reality. This can lead to straying from partnerships, having crushes, or idol and hero worship from afar. If we wish we can create our perfect dream lover or enjoy our sexual fantasies through dream incubation. Furthermore, if we have leanings towards sexual perversion we can indulge them in the dream state where there are no limits.

First examine your current love dreams if you have them. Is your dream lover always tall, dark and handsome, blond, exotic or do you have a variety? How does he or she compare with your real partner? What is different in the early stages with your dream lover? Do you encourage and participate or does your lover have to do all the foreplay? What turns you on and helps you reach a climax? Re-living our dream fantasies when making love can heal our sex life, make our bodies wake up and start to respond again, promoting unexpected and pleasurable responses from our partners. Sometimes we would rather not face our fears and prejudices and we hide from them.

Follow the seeding procedure, making notes on all the attributes you would like to find in this person. Draw a picture if you can. Don't use pictures of real people since it can be possible to make contact in the dream state and we have no right to invade the lives of others. They rarely live up to our expectations anyway and we could be in for a big disappointment. Instead, create your own special person. This will stimulate your sexual energy and greatly enhance your love life.

Just before sleeping create in your mind the most ideal

place for lovemaking. Now create your most wonderful sexual partner with whom to slowly and sensuously enjoy a most ecstatic night of love. As you fall asleep, your dreams will take over these images and you will have the most exquisite and magical experiences. Just think of the possibilities if such a dream should become lucid. You just won't want to get out of bed in the morning.

This often takes some practice and initially you can get some unexpected companions. You may find yourself with some unfanciable wimp whom you have to send on his way. If this happens, start the whole process over again from the beginning. Just persevere and things will soon improve. If you are feeling sex-starved or are in enforced celibacy, dream lovers bring untold bliss. Also there are times in a good relationship when we feel the need for a bit of variety. By taking a dream lover we don't spoil things with our partners. Go ahead and have fun.

Sexual diversions or perversions in dreams should not be feared. It is possible for the most normal of us to wonder about such things at times. In the dream state we do no one any harm, but we do have the opportunity to explore why we need such dreams. Are we distorting something that should be pleasurable into something sadistic or masochistic? Or are we, in fact, hiding from that part of our nature?

Pregnancy and birth can be related to sex and sexual needs but generally any form of gestation and birth is related to creativity. However, if there is an underlying fear of the consequences of sexual behaviour, then painful birthing, damaged or premature babies, sickness in pregnancy and losing your svelte figure can all indicate this fear and explain frigidity or impotence. Dreaming of contraceptives is usually a strong warning to take care. It need not necessarily have sexual connotations, being applicable to any form of protection.

Rape demonstrates a personal invasion of some sort or something being forced on us. It is about taking advantage of weaknesses, taking something by force or obliging a person to act against their will. It should always be examined from both points of view, since frequently we only see it from the feminine side. Sometimes symbolically raping a person's deep held views has a validity of its own.

My brother is watching me undress and I am ignoring him. Suddenly he grabs me and tries to kiss me. I struggle but know I can't get away. I feel disgusted at what he is trying to do to me.

Being watched undressing shows that you feel exposed and rape indicates that unwanted and unpleasant things are being forced on you. It is time for you to start taking charge of your life.

Nudity

Dreams of nudity are extremely common because they are to do with vulnerability. They occur when we fall short of our goals or the standards that others set for us and are found out or think we have been found out. The dream mind emphasizes our exposure. Nudity can also indicate naïveté, a juvenile approach, or a lack of preparation leading to being caught unaware. In this category also come dreams of being caught with our pants down or with our zip unfastened, or sitting on the loo when the door bursts open or the walls fall down.

Often in dreams of being naked everyone is aware of our condition. This shows that in our waking lives we are making fools of ourselves, even though we may not be aware of this. Sometimes, however, no one seems to notice. This indicates that our fears of what others are thinking are our own unfounded projections, and are generally very far from the truth, so there is really nothing to worry about. On other occasions when we are nude, people are looking and we simply don't care. This shows that we have shed outmoded restrictions or attitudes.

Sometimes we see others naked which shows that we can penetrate behind their façades. Their reactions in the dream show how aware they are. Sometimes we see the equivalent of the 'The Emperor's New Clothes' where he was unaware he was nude and everyone flattered and admired him. Unwittingly, he was the fool. These could also be aspects of ourselves.

In the main, clothing represents our outside image. How many hours and how much money do we spend on how we look? Consider how we dress for different occasions and situations. There are, of course, times when being naked feels really good, unencumbered and relaxing.

11

....

Understanding Our Dreams (4) – The Mansion of the Soul

I n Chapter 3 we encountered Jung's description of us as living in a beautiful house – the mansion of the soul. And this is what homes or houses usually represent in our dream world. They are the protective structures which we have built up around ourselves since birth, the way we appear to the outside world. Many interpreters relate the interiors of these houses to our bodies. They can also represent the mental and emotional side of our lives, the absolute total of all we believe in.

The home in a dream might appear as any of the types of house that can be found in **towns and cities**. These can range from elegant mansions to council houses, from regency terraces to slums, from smart apartments to hovels and tin shacks, with all the immense variety of possibilities in between. These houses represent ourselves in relationship with others, with a certain interdependency, yet at the same time being self-contained.

Country houses, however, present in two main ways. They are generally detached houses, either very well spaced out or quite closely huddled together. The latter are found in villages, grouped together for the common good. Other country houses range from castles and country estates to mudhuts and caves. Caves usually indicate the womb.

I am fascinated by a low, thatched cottage which fills me with fear although I recognize it. My mother gets sucked in. I feel relieved that this happens to her not me, but then she is back and I get sucked in.

The old cottage shows the problem is long-seated, probably related to the dreamer's youth because of its age and the presence of the mother. Something old often means being run-down and tired. The dreamer obviously wants his mother to take responsibility for his difficulties so sucks her in, trying to use her energy. This won't work, however, as she is spewed up and the dreamer is forced to confront this situation.

Then there is the **moveable home**. Here we have caravans, mobile homes, vardos, houseboats, tepees, tents, igloos and straw houses. Each, in its own way, indicates a different attitude to living. They show a form of rootlessness or being in transit, an unwillingness to be permanently tied. From a health point of view, they indicate avoiding an issue.

The **state of repair** of a building is important. This represents the façade we present to the outside world. If a house is in immaculate condition and in good repair, this is a good omen. Ruins speak for themselves. Any house with a flaw in it can be an indication of a physical problem. A house that is dilapidated, in need of a coat of paint, with the doors and windows falling off their hinges, means we need to look to our depression levels, our skin condition and how much exercise we are taking.

There are also the **places of learning** – schools, universities and museums which are about lessons in life that need to be learned; **places of entertainment** such as theatres, circuses and funfairs, which all indicate a façade, something that is not what it appears to be or putting on a brave face. Have we looked behind our own mask? Places of restriction, for example prisons or jails, tell the dreamer to look for parts of the body that are blocked or bursting out.

I was in a large department store. People were giving a man things to sell for them. I stood by the stand holding some biscuits. The man picked one, ate it and said it was very nice. I was supposed to talk to him later but didn't.

The dreamer here is in a place of choice where they can sell their talents to improve their lot. However, their talents are being used to nourish others rather than themselves. The dreamer could change this but decides not to bother. This is a dream of inaction, and the dreamer would be well advised to check his abdomen.

Places of worship usually feature in the more profound dreams and imply we are touching higher levels of ourselves. **Churches** and **cathedrals** tend to be the accumulation of all our spiritual beliefs. We often feel in awe and conscious of other beings or energies which touch us deeply. We usually experience extreme peace or go into meditation. If these places are damaged, they show neglect in the head area. Graveyards can be fearful places or might show a need to contact things from our past. It might also mean that part of the body is 'dying', so a check-up would be advisable.

I was really upset and found myself in what appeared to be a church. There were a few people who ignored me. I climbed several flights of dusty stairs in the tower, hoping to get a better view.

The dreamer here is looking for comfort, but being an unbeliever or a rare visitor is not greeted. Routes for advice are available, but are dusty and little used.

Temples can be ancient and huge edifices, simple earthworks or clumps of trees. These have a much more ritualistic feel, and often feelings of expectancy. There can also be a suggestion of sacrifice, combined with sensations of power or powerlessness. Check the heart, throat and stomach – all areas attacked in sacrifice.

Roofs are particularly important since they represent our protection against the storms of life. If they are falling in, maybe things are about to crash down around us. A leaking roof suggests that we are surrounded by irritations which are affecting us emotionally. We need to get up on the roof and attend to our aspirations.

Chimneys symbolize a link with higher levels. Frequently they are unused, blocked, or missing altogether. Thus the hearth fire cannot survive since there is no draught to carry our energy skywards. Good ventilation is crucial. The dreamer should check for any kind of respiratory ailment.

The **access** to the home is important. How many obstacles do you encounter leading up to your house in your dream? Are you keeping the world at bay and not allowing it access to you? On the other hand, if you have been too accessible, maybe the dream is telling you to put up a few barriers. It can also be a clear demonstration of our limitations, suggesting that the dreamer is worn out through an inability to say 'no'.

The same applies to **doors**, **shutters**, **curtains** and **windows**. It is good to be welcoming and not shut yourself away, but sometimes it is important to close windows and bolt doors securely to avoid being so vulnerable.

A friend calls me from an upstairs window and advises me to be careful about things. At my flat I am frightened to find the lock has disappeared. I look round but nothing has been taken.

This dreamer is being guided from a higher level, and so needs to pay attention. The missing lock shows inadequate protection, and suggests a weakened immune system.

I returned home to find the door unlocked and people in the house. I told them to empty their pockets and leave.

The dreamer here resents people intruding into her life, but only shows mild irritation. This could represent viruses that have been overcome.

Passing through doors, gates and other forms of barrier can also indicate moving to another level of consciousness. Be aware of this.

I was led up some stairs into a magistrate's court with people sitting at desks. Then we went through a wrought iron gate to the third floor. There were three balls which started to juggle.

The dreamer is being led to explore their problems, but needs to make clear judgements before progressing further. They can thus reach another threshold where things may have to be juggled for the right outcome. It could mean a necessary trip to hospital.

If you are outside the **front of the house**, make a note of the details of what you see. For example, does the house have an open look (open curtains and windows, door ajar, a welcoming garden)? Is it in good repair? What about the roof and chimney – do they give good protection? It might have a closed appearance, with all doors and windows closed, shuttered, draped or curtained. The front door might be around the side of the house. Maybe there is no chimney, suggesting no connection to higher levels. Maybe the whole place needs repairing and decorating. All these descriptions represent the dreamer's mental, emotional and physical state. Are we well balanced or deeply depressed?

The front door leads to a place of transition, the **hall**. Whenever we find ourselves here in a dream, we know we are at a moment of choice. Coming in indicates we are leaving the world outside and can choose which room to enter. Going out shows a commitment and a decision made.

The **kitchen** is often the first port of call. Kitchens are about nourishment on all levels, the need to nourish ourselves physically or spiritually, but equally to starve ourselves. It is also a creative place for mixing lots of different ingredients. Consider how this dream kitchen manifests. Is it like Old Mother Hubbard's with empty cupboards? This could mean that your current life is sterile and that you need to do something about it. On the other hand the dream could be about overeating, indicating that a few days fasting would be constructive. In both cases, a lack of love is obvious. Also check your digestive system.

If the kitchen is full to overflowing, again consider both sides of the coin. It could be that love is overflowing, that you have lots to give and should start sharing. Or it could mean that a time of fasting would be appropriate. Are you becoming either overweight or too thin?

Kitchens are also about food for thought, and can mean that you have reached a point in your life when you should consider things in more depth. They are also cosy, snug and safe places, where you don't have to hide behind a façade. They are places for sharing the proverbial cup of tea. They are also quite creative places – places for expressing ourselves without pretence. However, cleanliness should be examined. Could we be contaminating ourselves or others? Is what we have to offer stale or going putrid? Are we sharing the soiled side of ourselves? Are we offering poison?

Back doors are fairly private and away from the public eye, often leading directly from the kitchen into the **garden**. While the dream kitchen is about nourishment, the garden is our secret and safe place. Although for some, it can be a hard, uninviting place, full of rubbish. Many of us have a 'secret garden' in our lives. It is a mental image of a safe and beautiful place usually enclosed and accessible only to ourselves. No one can enter without invitation. It is a place for meditation and for retreat, where we can lick our wounds and recharge. This is a particularly good background for a seeding image.

Again we need to consider the contents of the garden. If it is mainly vegetables then, like the kitchen, it is a place of sustenance. If it is excessively orderly and neat, or wild, it again shows our character. It is worth remembering that weeds are only plants growing in what we consider to be the wrong place. If it is overgrown, maybe you haven't been visiting it lately, so are neglecting the recharging process.

With **basements and cellars**, we usually have to go down-stair. They are the places where we push all our unwanted things, particularly the unpleasant ones. Everything that we would prefer to forget or hide is hidden down there. Quite often in dreams we are filled with dread as we approach the cellar. We don't want to confront all those moments of intense embarrassment, or the times when we cheated, stole, swore, lusted, or lied. Those things we definitely do not want the world to know about are hidden in the cellar. We turn them into monsters, push them down and keep the door firmly locked. They are the stuff of nightmares and recurring dreams.

However, the dream mind won't allow us the luxury of ignoring them, especially in our moments of weakness. Thus, when a vulnerable situation arises during our waking hours, the unconscious opens the cellar door in our sleep. The only way to empty the cellar of nasties is to confront them, acknowledge them and come to terms with them, realizing that honesty is the best cure. We also need to examine our physical elimination processes. Are we constipated?

As always, however, there is another aspect to basements and cellars. They are also storage places for things of value such as coal and fuel to heat the house. There are often goods waiting to be recycled and many practical items. And what about the wine! Sometimes dreaming of a cellar shows the need to go within ourselves to make contact with our innate wisdom or even to hibernate for a while.

Living rooms represent current circumstances, especially in relation to those around us. Special attention should be paid here to the general level of homeliness. Is the place inviting and lived in? Is it excessively neat and tidy? Is it so untidy that walking across the floor resembles an assault course? Is it covered with dust sheets? The state of the room can give us a clear indication of the state of our life. It is also very much to do with the heart and all its functions.

I am in a big room of an old house, empty except for a fireplace and a big packing case. I feel there's a dead body in the case and it is my fault.

The room is dominated by the packing case because this problem is so large in the dreamer's life. It contains something that the dreamer thought was dead and buried long ago. It needs confronting so that he can come to terms with it and free himself totally. The fireplace shows that help is available from higher levels. This again can relate to the heart and possibly a condition which the dreamer thought was cured.

The **dining room** is slightly different from the kitchen in that it is about more formal nourishment, often on a grander scale. It could be to do with a need to create an impression on others. It is a place for assimilation, digestion and communication. On the other hand it can be cold and uninviting, with such formality or sparsity that we feel rejected.

Although a **study** is normally a workplace, in the dream context it is worth considering the true meaning of the word, which is to explore, learn and retain. This can apply equally to a **library**. However, the latter could mean that you need to locate a particular book or even write your own. This could also be telling you to find out now what may be wrong physically.

Stairs, **escalators** and **lifts** can be about transition but can also relate to life's journey. In this context they indicate changing levels. They show whether we can safely make it up or down, and offer opportunities to make contact with the deeper parts of ourselves. Be conscious of which parts of the house are being linked. It may be indicating one of the body's systems by connecting apparently unrelated health problems.

I tried to climb some stone stairs which suddenly changed to descending stairs. As I walked down they changed again and I was outside. The stone steps were worn and had weeds growing through them. The stairs were like those in the illusion where you could go down or up indefinitely in a circle.

Each time the dreamer thinks she has made it to a new level of achievement, she is back on the treadmill. She is caught in a vicious circle. The weeds show this is a long-standing problem. The time has come to make a break.

I find myself standing on top of a large ladder. A friend at the bottom starts to shake it and asks me to come down. I ask him to stop but he ignores me. He has a sharp knife with which he has been peeling vegetables and has a bag of fresh celery. I wake up frightened.

The dreamer has been working their way up the ladder of life and now finds someone is shaking their foundations. The friend is telling the dreamer to cut away some of the dross and stop ignoring the basic necessities of life. The dreamer is afraid to descend to his level in case he loses status. Alternatively this dream could be about the need for an operation.

Bathrooms are all about cleansing. They provide an opportunity to examine the dirt and dross that we have accumulated on all levels of our being. By using imagery to externalize, we are enabled to wash away negativity. We are all familiar with Lady Macbeth's 'Out damned spot! Out, I say!'. This can symbolize some disease or attitude. Dripping taps can indicate irritating persistence. Be conscious of any effort required to get clean and also whether you are washing yourself down the plug hole. This is clearly related to the urinary system.

Methods of washing can also carry some significance. Luxuriating in a bath can be quite different from taking a shower or having a 'lick and a promise'. Also the temperature of the water can be important. Warm is not necessarily indicative of pleasure and could occasionally indicate that we need warming up. A cold shower or a cooling bath usually have unpleasant associations, unless you have got yourself into a hot spot and either you, or the situation, needs cooling down. Fevers or hot flushes could be indicated.

I was having a bath and through the door I saw my brothers running away from a large dinosaur. I wondered what to do, so hid under the bed.

Having a bath here suggests the dreamer is washing his hands of a situation, but instead of fading away it is assuming very large proportions. The brothers running away shows a lack of external support. Beds are not good protection from dinosaurs – the dreamer must confront the problem alone in the end.

Lavatories, **toilets** and **restrooms** are about relieving ourselves and releasing things that have been adequately processed and are no longer required. If we get the message the result is amazing. Just think of the relief of going when you have been 'bursting for a pee'! Such dreams are frequently connected with stress and tension in our daily lives. However, urinating can simply be a physical need translated into the dream, as can wetting the bed.

Defecating is to do with eliminating unwanted memories or experiences. Strangely, it is often associated with wealth – for example, filthy lucre and the saying 'where there's muck, there's money'!

I dreamed that I was in the lavatory and that I was covered in excrement and couldn't find anything to clean myself. I went outside and every room was filled with the stuff. It was disgusting.

It transpired the following day that, after protracted legal proceedings, the dreamer's divorce was finalized and she was to receive a very large settlement – more money than she had ever had in her life.

I am looking for a toilet. I eventually find one that is outside the cubicle with no privacy. I look for another toilet and find one that is even more public, set on a stage and very well lit.

Loss of privacy shows some sort of threat and going to the toilet shows a need to relieve oneself of the burdens and problems of life. The dreamer recognizes this but is not strong enough to act. Being under the spotlight is unbearable and the dreamer feels that everyone can see through them.

If in your dreams you are locked out of the toilet, it can indicate that you are unable to release your problems. The same can apply when you can't find a toilet anywhere.

In the early part of our lives **bedrooms** are generally a place of secrets, the place where we go and lock the door and do what we please. They are, therefore, to do with escapism, private indulgences and fantasies. Later in life we allow them to be invaded when we take a partner, and then the sexual element comes in. If we are sharing a dream bedroom, very careful note should be made of the other occupants. These dreams can relate to malingering or sexual difficulties.

I dreamed that I was trying to make the bed after having made love to my husband, but the base sheet was in small squares which I was trying to fit together so that certain marks would not show. I became aware that my mother-in-law was sitting in the corner of the room looking disapproving, wearing a baby's nappy and sucking her thumb.

It transpired that this dreamer had real problems with her mother-in-law who disapproved of her as a wife for her son. She lived with them and quite clearly indicated to them that she thought sex was dirty. They were inhibited by the fear that she would hear them. She frequently resorted to childish and helpless behaviour to get sympathy and to keep them apart.

Attics and lofts are storage places but usually represent a more spiritual level, where we preserve our higher thoughts for future use. In the main, they appear neglected in dreams because so many of us nowadays have foregone the intuitive and inspirational in favour of the material and mundane sides of life. So when we arrive in the dream attic, it is often covered with dust and cobwebs. It is important to explore this area and truly understand any objects that you unearth. Also try to clean the windows and let some light in so that you can see.

All the rooms are excessively messy. A friend appears and is really rude about the untidiness, especially on the upper floors, saying I obviously cannot manage on my own. I had better clean up. Then she offers to help me.

The time has come for the dreamer to tidy her life to make room for something new. The friend is giving the dreamer a warning to protect herself. This is to do with immunity and the possible need for vaccinations.

12

....

Understanding Our Dreams (5) – More Dream Symbols

Our Journey through Life

One of the major themes to look for in our dreams is journeying, because this refers to our journey through life. If we look carefully travelling is almost always present in some form, whether on land, at sea or in the air. How you travel is significant. This will frequently give a clue about health problems (*see* Chapter 8). If you are short of breath on your journey or if your feet are sore, look for the connections.

Whether we are riding a horse or in any sort of vehicle – be it on land, sea or in the air – the important question is who is driving. If it is you, then you need to consider what you are driving and in what manner. Are you in charge or are you being taken for a ride? This point is crucial since so often in life we are being manipulated by others without realizing it. For dream healing this is a very important symbol. We need to bring our disease under control.

If you are **horseback riding** and the horse is galloping off with you or bucking you off, a really powerful energy is at work and you certainly aren't in charge. If the horse is going calmly in hand, responding to your every command, it shows that you have this powerful energy at your fingertips.

Cars of all varieties represent our personalities (and to a certain extent our bodies), to which there are many facets. It is quite remarkable how much information can be gleaned simply by examining a dream car. Pay attention to the type. Sometimes we dream of being in a sexy sports car but more often it is a sedate saloon. It is not necessary to list lots of interpretations for the different shapes, brands and sizes, because with a little common sense you will get the inference. However, bear in mind that foreign makes of car indicate that you could be in a foreign environment, that there is something alien at work, or that there is something wrong with your body.

Colour is usually quite important since it indicates how flashy or unobtrusive you wish to be (*see* page 148). The same can apply to the type of roof (convertible or enclosed sedan). Is it a two-seater or multi-seater? The condition of the car is also significant. Is it new, ordinary, old, rusty, dirty, highly polished? Any of these factors can be applied to our personalities. The same applies to the ability of the engine to propel. Does it fire first time, is it in good order or is it always breaking down?

Another feature is whether we change cars in our dreams. Are we swapping from car to car, in other words trying on different images, or do we stick with the same model until it falls to pieces? In fact, is it time we took it to the breaker's yard? All this applies to any other type of vehicle – boats, airplanes, bikes, and so on.

Having considered all these externals, is it moving or is it stationary – simply not going anywhere? Has it stopped for a good reason? If you are driving, it infers that you are taking an active part in your life. If you are a passenger be wary, especially if there is no driver. Try to ascertain who might be driving your personality. Are you constantly being pushed to one side or are you happy to be driven? Could it be that you are a back-seat driver, in which case, who have you let take the wheel, who do you want to run your life for you or are you just being bossy?

Finally, is there a driver at all? Is there, in fact, anyone in control? Maybe you are not even in the car. Is it simply parked or has it been taken over by others? These are very useful symbols for visualizations to incubate into dreams.

With **public transport**, we give over the responsibility of our progress to others, perhaps representing a doctor or a hospital. Using public transport in a dream can be simply for our own convenience so does not necessarily have an immense significance, but on the other hand it could show that we are allowing the establishment to run our lives. This could be holding us in a rut, preventing free expression. Or, of course, it could simply be keeping us on track, preventing us from going off the rails. Look for this when any kind of **rail** is involved – tram, train, monorail, trolleybus, and the like.

Next our progress needs to be examined. Having passed up the responsibility, where are we being taken? Is it somewhere we want to go? Who is in control of the situation? Are we moving freely or is the traffic snarled up? Is the weather interfering? Or is everything going swimmingly?

Examine the different types of **propulsion**. Firstly, we have our **own two feet** and our own efforts. Secondly, there are **natural forces**, namely wind and air currents, water with rapids and waves, snow with avalanches and ice, earth with landslides, earthquakes and eruptions, and gravity itself. Thirdly, we have **animal power**, either carrying us or pulling us. Finally, we have the man-made variety, the **engine**. And, of course, we can have combinations of these features.

To understand these is again simple once we realize that on foot or using our own physical means, we are responsible. With natural forces, we are often at their mercy, no matter how clever we think we are, but we can harness them to a certain extent. The same applies to animal power but it is important here to realize that there are two minds at work. With the last category, the engine, we should be in control, but often we are not.

Direction is the next important point, since it is about taking us to our goals. Is the road ahead easy or filled with potholes? Can we see where we are going? Are we going off at a tangent, round in circles, or simply meandering? Clearly this could relate to the way we live our lives. Consider different ways of moving. These can all be applied to our life journey.

Getting lost, taking the wrong bus or train or connection, is a regular theme. They all reflect having no clear direction or persistently going the wrong way. Such dreams can be a cry for help, so pay attention to them.

A really common theme is that of missing the bus, train or connection. This is pointing out lost opportunities, missed chances, overdoing things and running out of time. Such dreams are encouraging us to open our eyes and stop throwing away all our chances. They can also suggest we stop worrying since there will usually be another opportunity along shortly.

The final consideration about journeys is **impediments**. How often does our transport malfunction – refuse to start, start and then stall, run out of fuel, break down, get a puncture, blow up, steam up, freeze up, have brake failure, come off the rails, become becalmed, get caught in quicksand, fall down a hole, sink or take off with us? Again this is very much about being in or out of control and is simple to interpret when you see the connection between the images and the journey through life. However, do not forget that a hold-up could have a beneficial effect. What about accidents? Are we on a collision course or is someone trying to collide with us? Have we been idle about keeping things in good repair?

Another hindrance is the different types of **barrier**. For example, a wall can represent current problems inhibiting our growth. The wall can be new, indicating that our current barrier is new, old, showing the problem has been around for a long time, or crumbling, indicating just that. There may be a way through, round or over the barrier, or it may be impenetrable. Maybe you feel you could just knock it down anyway. On the other side is the future. If we can see over the wall, is there anything there? If there is nothing, then we have created nothing; if there is something, how does it look? If you can't see over the wall it is because you are not yet ready to look, or are maybe too obsessed by your current difficulties.

Other types of barrier include chasms, road blocks, barriers, gates, rivers, sea, fire, doors, guards, guard dogs and dead-ends, to mention a few. A barrier is anything which gets in the way.

Animals

From time immemorial mankind has been using animals as metaphors for human behaviour. We are also animals and express similar habits and instincts. Thus they can be said to represent our instinctual side. Herding and flocking instincts are easy to recognize in the human. People tend to cling together for group security, and to participate in activities because everyone else is doing them. Rather than stick out like a sore thumb, we want to match and blend. We succumb like animals to the pecking order. We know our place in the hierarchy and when we overstep the mark and throw our weight around, we are cuffed back into place like any other young pup.

Animals in dreams can be aspects of ourselves or represent emotions, fears or possibilities. Take, for example, a dream about walking a dog. Dream **dogs** usually mean friends. If the dog is in charge and pulling like mad on the leash, it shows that either we are being dragged through life by our friends, or that we are being held back from our rightful roles. Animals are also renowned as dream guides and helpers.

Wild animals indicate a sense of freedom but also untamed instincts. They can be a warning that we need more discipline to live within our self-imposed civilization. **Domesticated animals**, on the other hand, show amenability, or a preparedness to work for the common good. **Caged or penned animals** fall somewhere between the two, since sometimes they are wild, whilst others have been bred in captivity. **Pets** show a caring side to our natures but they can also suggest we are being patronizing.

Animals are connected with the shape-shifting skills of the shaman on the inner planes. He usually has his own particular animal guide who protects and leads him and stays with him through thick and thin. At other times his spirit can take on the energy of a particular animal, using its instinctual features to alleviate a difficult situation. An example of this comes from a friend of mine who dreamed that she was being attacked unfairly by a friend at work. Because the dream was lucid, she changed herself into a tiger and frightened her tormentor. After that she had little further trouble at work.

All the things we do to and for animals represent how we are treating ourselves or those around us. They are self-explanatory.

Take, for example, bridles, halters, reins, saddles, collars, leads and lead reins, chains, hobbles, nose rings; caging, penning, herding, trapping, hunting; bathing, brushing, feeding, shearing, branding, nursing, whipping – many of these words are used as metaphors in our everyday language. In every dream instance we need to consider whether we are doing it to ourselves or to those around us.

Amphibians, which live on land and in water, and creatures such as **fish** or **lobsters**, which live permanently in water, are invariably related to the emotions or things surfacing or emerging from the unconscious. So if we dream of fish, something which is slippery or elusive or even fishy is stirring and trying to attract our attention.

Birds can be gregarious or solitary. They represent flocking, migratory instincts, and the ability to travel great distances. They can be messengers, or alternatively they can be watchers. They take an overview, being able to observe from considerable heights.

Colours

Most dreams are in colour but generally we are not particularly aware of this unless some aspect is brought to our attention. Colours create atmospheres and can have an overall livening or muting effect. So if, for example, there is a dominance of red there are two possible interpretations. Either we are lacking in energy and stimulation or we have too much. This can apply equally to our surroundings or our clothing in a dream. The dream is emphasizing our need to take in the significance of that colour.

If the colours in your dream are particularly vivid and dramatic, then it could be a precognitive dream, although this is not a foolproof guarantee. Dreaming in black and white is fairly common and often has no significance. Sometimes, though, it can mean that your life has become colourless or that the dream is about the past, before Technicolor was invented.

If when you dress in the morning you feel a certain colour does absolutely nothing for you and makes you look flat and dull, replace it immediately with a colour which makes you glow. Not making the change can lead to feeling low all day, almost as though you have reduced your immunity and become vulnerable. What we wear and how we feel tones in with our aura, the multi-coloured energy field surrounding our body. Your dreams can show you that, through bad use of colour, you are deflating yourself.

The seven colours of the spectrum, plus black and white, all have marked significance in dreams and research has shown that they can strongly influence how we react. Some schools of thought include magenta which lies between red at one end of the spectrum and violet at the other and can be seen in a prism. There are many secondary and tertiary colours, but the meanings for the ten major colours are fairly standard.

Red is the basic colour and is to do with raw energy. This can be interpreted as strength to carry out manual tasks, vitality, willpower, stimulation and motivation. On the other hand it can symbolize anger, frustration, revenge, impatience or embarrassment and blushing. People who wear red tend to be very physical, expressing themselves through their bodies. Related metaphors include red rag to a bull; I saw red; to become red in the face; scarlet woman; red as blood; red as a rose. Lots of red in your healing dreams means that there is something fiery and explosive that needs immediate attention.

Orange is the colour of groups where the raw energy is blended and used for joint enterprises. It is about joining, expansion, sexuality, friendliness and sociability. It is also about fruitfulness and ripeness. It used to be the colour worn by condemned criminals and is used for the robes of the Bhuddist orders. Orange represents sociability or involvement in the community. Orange-tawny was a colour worn by money-lenders, while orange blossom is a symbol of fruitfulness for brides. A predominance of orange in a dream could indicate sexual or elimination problems or that mingling with other people is important.

Yellow relates to intellect, self-discipline, mental discrimination and detachment, and its converse side is excessive criticism, cynicism, fear, jealousy and adultery. Yellow is often equated with gold which is an expression of achievement. It is also connected with the digestion and also digesting information. In common usage, yellow seems to have negative attributes so consider it carefully: yellow belly; to have a yellow streak. The French used to daub yellow on the doors of traitors, while Judas is often portrayed in yellow.

Green is to do with love, harmony, generosity and nurturing. It can represent being young, fresh and immature. It is thought to be the colour of healing and growth. Conversely it represents inexperience and jealousy and can be muting and depressing. Related metaphors are green round the gills; green with envy; green behind the ears; as green as grass; green fingers; a greenhorn; going green. In some cultures it is deemed to be unlucky to wear green. It is much more common to wear it nowadays, but it could be explained as the colour of blending or camouflage.

Blue is the colour of peace, but also of authority and teaching. Patience, nurturing, forgiveness and understanding are also attributes. Conversely it can be thought cold, isolated, detached, passive or depressed. It is frequently connected with communication and vocal expression. This is the standard colour for uniforms, representing conforming or being made to conform. Metaphors include being true blue; in a blue mood; feeling blue; turning blue; a blue-stocking; blue blood; once in a blue moon; the blues (music); blue films.

Indigo is related to intuition and the ability to foresee or divine, or conversely to pure logic or obtuseness. It represents beauty and asceticism. It is useful for healing eye problems. This is really the colour of twilight and early dawn, times of transition when one's awareness can lead to heightened perception. The colour is not commonly worn.

Violet/purple is about inspiration, meditation, spiritual consciousness and religion. In its pinker tones, it indicates love and compassion. Its opposite features are an inability to live in the present, being spaced-out, day-dreaming and isolation. In its darker tones it is worn by royalty and the clergy but is becoming more and more popular in all its shades as a spiritual colour. Metaphors include retiring as a violet; it's raining violets; shrinking violet; purple prose.

Magenta indicates organizing, the ability to take oneself in hand and altruism. It is about administration and running large organizations. Its opposite is complete disorganization and incompetence. It is really the spiritual side of red, and is thus a blending of the material with the higher mind.

White is a combination of all the colours of the spectrum. It signifies purity, innocence, unsullied things, virginity, simplicity and candour. Alternatively, it can be blinding or dazzling, preventing us from seeing clearly. It is commonly worn as a symbol of innocence and purity by brides, novices and babies, and also to offset the strength of other colours. When feeling under the weather, white can be a sympathetic colour to wear for most people. However, if you are excessively pale it doesn't work, so try something bright. Metaphors include white as snow; white in the eye; white as a swan; white as a sheet; white elephants; white feather; white horses; white lies.

Black is really the absence of colour. It is connected with mourning, death and funerals. It is associated with night, fear and the mysterious, but also with hatred and vindictiveness, gloom and depression. It can also be a shade of great comfort and retreat, representing being snug in the dark. It is generally worn to conform – the uniform, the dark suit, the little black dress. Alternatively it can evoke strong passions and fears in the sensuous dress or the all-covering cloak. Metaphors include black as night; black as death; black as ink; blacklist or black balled; black letter day; black books; black sheep. In dreams it can mean being in shadow and should be treated as of significance.

•••••••••••••••••••••••••

The Way Forward

Where do we go from here? If at all possible, join a dream group as dream sharing is incredibly therapeutic. The mere act of talking about your dream to another person will make things that you had previously overlooked rise to the surface. Sharing within a group can be fascinating, so long as everyone is prepared to be completely honest when it comes to interpretation and say what they think, however stupid it may seem. It is often the silliest comment that sparks an answer for us.

When you are dream sharing you also have a chance to become more aware of the language that you use for description. Chapter 5 discussed the use of visual, aural and kinesthetic words. Furthermore by repeating the dream we often experience again the physical sensations and emotions which we may have overlooked in our journal record.

In a group environment we can often come to terms more easily with our hidden agendas and secondary gains through examining our approach to the group and the amount of sharing we are prepared to do.

If there is no local group, why not start your own? You will be surprised how many people will be interested. Find a quiet, warm and comfortable venue that is easily accessible. Decide how often you will meet. Some people do not like to be too tied, preferring fortnightly or monthly sessions. Longer gaps are better since they allow for more dreaming time between meetings. Patterns can emerge and connections can be made with people and features in your life.

If there has to be a small charge for the room (or for lighting, heating, and so on) get members to pay up front. We are all full of good intentions; but, when the weather gets bad or we have more important demands on our time, groups such as these can peter out and the facilitator can be badly out of pocket.

Be sure to agree confidentiality, because some dreams can be very revealing, rendering the dreamer extremely vulnerable. Because of this, it is probably better to discourage note-taking.

If you have to work on your own, there are other things you can do. Firstly, you might like to indulge in some artistic expression of your dreams. Many poems have come into being this way. Alternatively, try drawing your dream. Pictures can replace thousands of words. You can also play a piece of music which you feel evokes the dream scene. Get up and move to the sound and let your emotions speak through the music. All these will give you clues to the health of your body, mind and spirit, and can be used to improve your life.

Finally it is worth pointing out that we all create our own futures. We are all aware, within certain parameters, of what we will be doing for the next hour or so. We have already created this in our minds. The same can be said for tomorrow and probably the whole of the next week. It shows that we do, in fact, have some control over what is going to happen to us. It can therefore be fun to plan the future we would like and create the goals we want to achieve. Take some pieces of paper and write the heading 'Me now' in the top left-hand corner of the first page. Then write your ultimate goal at the bottom right-hand corner of the last page. In between, insert as many pages as you like on which to write sensible, attainable steps. Make them little ones so you can succeed with them all. Each night you can work on this journey, sowing the seed for the next goal into your dream, working on the answer and recording it. At times you may need to divert, or put in an extra step as a result of your dreams. Often, as a result of such seeding, healing can be enhanced.

Happy Dreaming!

Bibliography

Andrews, Ted, *The Healer's Manual*, Llewellyn Publications, 1993

Angelo, Jack, *Spiritual Healing*, Element Books, 1991

Benor, Dr Daniel J, *Healing Research*, Vols 1 & 2, Helix Editions, 1992

Bergson, Henri, *Matter and Memory*, 1896

Bhagavad Gita, The (trans Juan Mascaro), Penguin Books, 1962

Braude, Stephen E, *The Limits of Influence*, Routledge & Kegan Paul, 1986

Brennan, Barbara Ann, *Hands of Light*, Bantam Books, 1987

Campbell, Joseph, *The Masks of God*, Vol 1, Arkana, 1991

Capra, Fritjof, *The Turning Point*, Flamingo, 1982

Castenada, Carlos, *The Art of Dreaming*, Aquarian Press, 1993

Cheiro (Count Louis Hamon), *Cheiro's Book of Numbers*, Herbert Jenkins, 1933

Chetwynd, Tom, *A Dictionary for Dreamers*, Aquarian Press, 1993

— *A Dictionary of Symbols*, Paladin, 1982

Chinkwita, Mary, *The Usefulness of Dreams: An African Perspective*, Janus Books, 1993

Chopra, Deepak, *Quantum Healing*, Bantam Books, 1989

Cooper, J C, *An Illustrated Encyclopaedia of Traditional Symbols*, Thames & Hudson, 1978

Dee, Nerys, *Discover Dreams*, Aquarian Press, 1989

— *Your Dreams & What They Mean*, Aquarian Press, 1984

Dethlefsen, Thorwald, *The Healing Power of Illness*, Element Books, 1990

Donahoe, James J, *Dream Reality*, Bench Press, 1974

Dossey, Larry, *Beyond Illness*, Shambhala Publications, 1984

Dunne, J W, *An Experiment With Time*, Faber & Faber, 1958

Drury, Nevill, *The Shaman and the Magician*, Arkana, 1982

Farraday Ann, *The Dream Game*, Temple Smith, 1975

— *Dream Power*, Hodder & Stoughton, 1972

Fontana, David, *Understanding Your Dreams*, Element Books, 1990

Frazer, J G, *The Golden Bough*, Macmillan Press, 1922

Gardner, Robert L, *The Rainbow Serpent*, Inner City Books, 1990

Gimbel, Theo, *Healing Through Colour*, C W Daniel, 1980

Goldsmith, Joel S, *The Infinite Way*, Unwin, 1979

Grimble, Arthur, *A Pattern of Islands*, John Murray, 1952

Hall, James A, *Patterns of Dreaming*, Shambhala Publications, 1977

Hay, Louise L, *You Can Heal Your Life*, Eden Grove, 1988

Hearne, Dr Keith, *The Dream Machine*, Aquarian Press, 1990

Hope, Murry, *The Psychology of Healing*, Element Books, 1989

Jung, Carl Gustav, *Man & His Symbols*, Picador, 1978

— *Memories, Dreams & Reflections*, Collins, 1963

— *Dreams*, Routledge & Kegan Paul, 1985

Koestler, Arthur, *The Sleepwalkers*, Arkana, 1989

LeBerge, Stephen, *Lucid Dreaming*, Ballantine Books, 1985

Leek, Sybil, *Dreams*, W H Allen, 1976

Linn, Denise, *A Pocketful of Dreams*, Judy Piatkus (Publishers) Ltd, 1988

Mabinogion, Everyman's Library, 1975

Matthews, Caitlin, *Arthur and The Sovereignty of Britain*, Arkana, 1989

Mindell, Arnold, *Dreambody*, Routledge & Kegan Paul, 1982

Nau, Dr Erika, *Huna Self Awareness*, Samuel Weiser, 1992

Peters, Dr Roderick, *Living With Dreams*, Rider, 1990

Playfair & Hill, *The Cycles of Heaven*, Souvenir Press, 1978

Pruyear, Herbert B, *The Edgar Cayce Primer*, Bantam Skylark, 1982

Rogo, D Scott, *Beyond Reality*, Aquarian Press, 1990

Reed, A W, *Aboriginal Legends*, Reed Books, 1978

Roberts & Mountford, *The Dawn of Time (Aboriginal Myths)*, Rigby Limited, 1969

Saint-Denys, Hervey de, *Dreams and How To Guide Them*, Duckworth & Co, 1982

Sams, Jamie & Carson, David, *Medicine Cards*, Bear & Co, 1988

Sharper Knowlson, T, *The Origins of Popular Superstitions & Customs*, Studio Editions Ltd, 1994

Storr, Anthony, *Jung – Selected Writings*, Fontana Press, 1983

Sutherland, Elizabeth, *Ravens and Black Rain*, Corgi Books, 1985

Tanner, Wilda B, *The Mystical, Magical, Marvelous World of Dreams*, Souvenir Press, 1988

Tao Te Ching, Ch'u Ta-Kao, Mandala, 1959

Upanishads, The, (trans Juan Mascaro), Penguin Books, 1965

Ullman, M, Krippner, S, and Vaughan, A, *Dream Telepathy*, Turnstone, 1973

van der Post, Laurens, *The Heart of the Hunter*, Odhams Press Ltd, 1961

von Franz, Marie-Louise, *The Feminine in Fairy Tales*, Shambhala, 1972

Watson, Lyall, *Gifts of Unknown Things*, Hodder & Stoughton, 1976

— *Supernature*, Hodder & Stoughton, 1973

Wilson, Colin, *The Occult*, Mayflower Books, 1973

Wolf, Fred Alan, *The Eagle's Quest*, Mandala, 1991

— *Parallel Universes*, Paladin, 1991

— *The Dreaming Universe*, Simon & Schuster, 1994

Young, Alan, *Spiritual Healing*, De Vorss, 1981

Useful
Addresses

AUSTRALIA
Australian College of Alternative Medicine
11 Howard Avenue, Mount Waverley, Victoria 3149

Australasian College of Natural Therapies
620 Harris Street, Ultimo, NSW 2007
Tel: 02212 6699

Australian Traditional Medicine Society
Suite 3, First Floor, 120 Blaxland Road, Ryde, NSW 2112
Tel: 612 808 2825
Fax: 612 809 7570

CANADA
Canadian Holistic Medical Association
42 Redpath Avenue, Toronto, Ontario M4S 2J6
Tel: 416 485 3071

UK
British Holistic Medical Association
179 Gloucester Place, London NW1 6DX
Tel: 0171 262 5299

157

The British Register of Complementary Medicine
PO Box 194
London SE16 1QZ
Tel/Fax: 0171 237 5175

The Centre for the Study of Complementary Medicine
51 Bedford Place, Southampton, Hampshire, SO15 2DT
Tel: 01703 334752
Fax: 01703 231835

The Institute for Complementary Medicine
Unit 15 Tavern Quay, Commercial Centre, Rope Street,
London, SE16 1TX
Tel: 0171 237 5165

USA
Alliance/Foundation for Alternative Medicine
160 NW Widmer Place, Albany, OR 97321
Tel: 503 926 4678

Holistic Health Association
PO Box 17400, Anaheim, CA 92817 7400
Tel: 714 779 6152

American Holistic Medical Association
4101 Lake Boone Trail, Suite 201, Raleigh, NC 27607
Tel: 919 787 5181

Index